'Whether you are an experienced mar[...] career, *Press Start* provides a useful over[...] of marketing – from Maslow's Hierarchy and the core motivational levers, to the modern complexity of human behaviour and a new tier of human needs. With tried and tested case studies, *Press Start* will set your goals and metrics, build a business case and develop your own marketing gamification strategy.'

Sarah Sherwin, Managing Director, Broad Street Communications Ltd.

'Marketing gamification is one of the best-kept business secrets of our times. *Press Start* is the insight-packed roadmap every marketer needs to unlock commercial rewards from gameplay in solving real-world customer problems.'

Tony Wood, Managing Director, X Factor Communications and Co-founder, Virgin Money

'*Press Start* provides thoughtful insight into the psychology of customer engagement, with a focus on how lessons from the world of games can generate ongoing customer loyalty. The book is a well-written, entertaining blueprint for marketers who would like to understand the opportunities of gamification, but also need to understand the pitfalls of bad game design. It is of particular relevance for marketers seeking to build on-going, multi-round, long-term relationships with their customers.'

Professor Kai Peters, Pro-Vice-Chancellor of Business & Law, Coventry University

'Fascinating. A must-read for anyone interested in applying gamification to marketing. I have been waiting for a book like this for a long time, and it's finally here.'

Jonah Berger, Associate Professor of Marketing, Wharton School of the University of Pennsylvania and author of Contagious: Why Things Catch On

'Play has created strong communities since the dawn of mankind. This ground-breaking book elegantly builds upon philosopher Huizinga's concept of purposeful play and seamlessly links it to neurobiological research, motivational theory and consumer behaviour. In this thoughtful and well-researched book, the authors have masterfully blended accessible theory with practical advice which will help the reader develop their own, detailed marketing gamification strategy.'

Dr Albert Zandvoort, Professor, HEC Paris Business School, Psychotherapist and Entrepreneur

'For anyone wanting to understand, apply and implement gamification when it comes to marketing, read this book. Dan and Albert leave no stone unturned, analysing motivation and psychological theories, providing real-life case studies, stories and principles, whilst providing you with a toolkit to design your own gamification solution to allow you to better connect with your clients and potential customers.'

Simon Heyes, founder, Novel

'For serious marketers only! If you are looking to integrate gamification into your marketing strategy, well, you've come to the right place. This is the bible. Finally a truly strategic approach to an often-times misunderstood practice.'

Joe Pulizzi, author of various books including Killing Marketing, Content Inc. and Epic Content Marketing

'*Press Start* is a particularly insightful book and easy read for anyone interested in game mechanics. Van der Meer and Griffin turn industry jargon into a practical and useful framework that can be applied to a multitude of business challenges right away.'

Thomas Clever, Managing Director and Co-Founder, Clever Franke

'It's easy to underestimate the power of games. However, challenges and rewards are effective tools for driving consumer loyalty and engagement. *Press Start* not only provides fascinating insights into this process, it also functions as an accessible and engaging guide to success.'

Nir Eyal, bestselling author of Hooked and Indistractable

'*Press Start* upends conventional thinking in marketing and goes a step further – hacking directly into aspects of human motivation and psychology to provide a genuinely revolutionary path to customer connection. Gamification is a megatrend that will soon be a determining factor in the success of marketing firms, and this is the *ur-text* to kick-start your gamification strategy.'

David Mayer, Leadership Partner in Data and Analytics, Gartner

PRESS START

Using Gamification to Power-up Your Marketing

Daniel Griffin & Albert van der Meer

BLOOMSBURY BUSINESS
LONDON · OXFORD · NEW YORK · NEW DELHI · SYDNEY

BLOOMSBURY BUSINESS
Bloomsbury Publishing Plc
50 Bedford Square, London, WC1B 3DP, UK

BLOOMSBURY, BLOOMSBURY BUSINESS and the Diana logo are
trademarks of Bloomsbury Publishing Plc

First published in Great Britain 2019

A catalogue record for this book is available from the British Library

Library of Congress Cataloguing-in-Publication data has been applied for

ISBN: 978-1-4729-7051-0; eBook: 978-1-4729-7049-7

2 4 6 8 10 9 7 5 3 1

Typeset by Deanta Global Publishing Services, Chennai, India
Printed and bound in Great Britain by CPI Group (UK) Ltd, Croydon CR0 4YY

To find out more about our authors and books visit www.bloomsbury.com
and sign up for our newsletters

Contents

Introduction

'*Gamification*'.

Both of us have stood at the front of hundreds of workshops, meetings and various other audiences and uttered that one word. And we can usually guess the initial response.

Sometimes we're lucky, and it's one of genuine interest and enthusiasm. But often it's a rolling of eyes, maybe even the cry of 'fad' or the occasional smirk. These are the tell-tale signs of people who have tried and failed to implement one of the most powerful motivational tools we have available to us, or worse, a sign that they never tried at all and just dismissed it because of too many negative opinions around it.

We get it, we've either seen it, been part of it or thought the same thing too. Both of us have been interested in gamification since it gained its first burst of mainstream popularity around 2012. We were both working at a business school at the time, and as avid gamers, we were both initially excited by the possibility of merging our favourite pastime with our professions.

We followed the same bandwagon and tried and failed at various implementations across marketing, HR and L&D over the years. We did what a lot of other people did at the time, we read a few guides and case studies online and blindly applied gamification to everything we could with no structure or strategy:

- 'Of course adding badges and points to our website will improve engagement'…
- 'If we just add a forum to this teaching portal, our students will start talking to each other'…
- 'Maybe if we add a leaderboard this might work'…

It was a new, shiny toy that we all just wanted to play with. And like all new, shiny toys, we got bored and moved on.

And gamification died, or at best, limped along, dragged by an army of consultants and experts who didn't want to lose their jobs or the industry niche they'd carved out for themselves.

Or at least that's what the majority of people think. The reality is that gamification never died; it just went undercover. This is especially true for our area of expertise, marketing gamification.

Why read this book?

Points, badges, leaderboards – these are the words you normally hear when anyone starts talking about marketing gamification, and that's usually when people stop listening. They've heard it before, didn't work for them then, won't work for them now.

But if we talk about eBay, Fitbit, LinkedIn, Duolingo or Booking.com and what tools and techniques these companies use to grow so successfully – then people start listening again.

The truth is, gamification is alive and well in marketing, but the success stories aren't apparent enough or have been rebranded as User Experience (UX) or Customer Experience (CX), as marketers try distancing themselves from a set of tools and techniques that people see as gimmicky or manipulative.

These marketers are customer focused; they have done the work to understand what their customers need from them and then looked for the best tools to engage with these customer needs. They found (either by accident or design) 'gamification'.

The difference is that rather than blindly applying tools with no strategy, they started with strategy first, and then tested a wide range of tools to see what worked and what didn't. There were no gimmicks, no silly games, and no paint-by-numbers approaches. They worked out how to do this without a guide, just like us.

But now you have a guide; this book. We'll show you real-life case studies and examples of how to apply gamification successfully to your own marketing through three sections:

- **Section 1:** Explains the theory behind what gamification is and why it is so important, then takes you through the various motivational and psychological theories relevant to marketing gamification.
- **Section 2:** Shows you which game mechanics (like points and badges) link to which motivational levers and provides real-life examples of how organisations have used them in their marketing.
- **Section 3:** Takes you through our practical framework to designing your own gamification solution, from segmenting your audience and setting goals, to building your own solution and reporting on it.

Why listen to us?

If you haven't worked it out yet, there are two of us writing this book.

Albert van der Meer is a creative consultant based in the Netherlands. His expertise lies specifically within narrative and visual entertainment, storytelling and teaching using this expertise. He draws gamification knowledge from his experience as a freelance filmmaker, media producer, expert blogger in game-based solutions and a team-building facilitator, working as a consultant with a great many international businesses, including Hult International Business School, England & Wales Cricket Board and UK Sport, to name but a few.

With these skills and this knowledge, he now helps businesses, educational institutions and other corporate organisations to improve team co-operation and develop deeper, more meaningful learning through the use of narrative and gameful design techniques. His main focus is in creating environments and experiences where individuals learn through adventure and fiction to gain interpersonal and leadership skills.

Dan Griffin is a professional marketer with over 10 years of experience working for international businesses such as online retail giant Amazon and international business schools, as well as numerous charities and small businesses. His practical experience across B2B and B2C marketing is backed up by theoretical knowledge from his CIM marketing qualifications, plus numerous individual and team awards from Amazon and The Learning and Performance Institute.

He is a multi-disciplined marketer but has gained extensive experience in digital marketing throughout his career, developing an interest in gamification when researching consumer psychology. Since then, he has deep-dived into the subject, testing multiple frameworks and ideas across various industries, gaining a comprehensive knowledge of what does and doesn't work from the frontlines.

Who is this book for?

We've written this book to guide you through creating your own marketing gamification solution.

In this book, we imagine that we're talking to a marketer in an organisation or a business owner who is looking for new ways to engage with their customers meaningfully. Someone who has tried the standard approaches to marketing but feels like there is something more, something missing from the online guides that the industry just shares back and forth.

You will have a genuine desire to engage with the people you do business with, and the understanding that building long-term relationships and trust with your customers is the best long-term strategy for your organisation. You will not be looking for a quick fix, because what we talk about in this book will not work for you if you are.

If this sounds like you – great! Welcome to the book. If it doesn't, know that this book has been written specifically for this type of person, so you may want to skip parts of the book that cover information you may already know, or that doesn't apply to you.

Lastly, three quick caveats

1) We cover a huge range of subjects in this book: gamification theory, motivational psychology, brain chemistry, marketing theory and marketing strategy to name just a few topics. Because of this, we cover what we think are the most relevant and need-to-know aspects of these topics and then move on to the next thing you need to know. We do not pretend to give a comprehensive analysis of entire subjects, so if you want to know more about something, we suggest either buying a book dedicated to it or going through our further reading section at the back of the book.

2) We also don't look at specific technologies or companies that provide the tools we discuss. This is because the industry is fast moving and we do not want to give advice that is out of date within just a few weeks of being released. What we do give you is the knowledge to apply the principles yourself and to be able to spot tools that can genuinely help you in the market.

3) Lastly, you should know that gamification won't be the right tool for every situation. It is particularly well suited for specific types of business and certain customer types, but we will explain all this throughout the book. That said, even if you read the entire book and decide gamification isn't for you, we're confident you will take away a better understanding of consumer psychology and a better method for targeting your customers with your marketing.

But enough caveats, on with the book!

SECTION ONE

Theory

There is unfortunately still a fair amount of scepticism around gamification. This is largely because it had a bubble around 2012 that burst after a lot of very public failures. This was only made worse over time as countless 'gurus' emerged with one-size-fits-all solutions that cemented gamification's reputation as a fad.

So why even bring it up again? Because gamification – especially in marketing – can be an incredibly effective tool, one that is used by many successful businesses across every industry. So we're going to show you how.

However, first, we need to agree on exactly what gamification is. This lack of a concrete definition is another reason why gamification is often ignored because not enough people understand it or they quickly oversimplify it. This is why we start by examining what gamification is, breaking down several experts' definitions and then providing our own fit-for-purpose definition that we will use throughout the rest of the book.

Next, we'll look at the gaming and gamification industry and talk about why it is such a relevant and important factor right now. There is a reason gamification took off when it did, and there is a reason why its growth has never really stopped. This is vital for you to understand if you're going to sell the idea of marketing gamification to the rest of your organisation; its increasing relevance cannot be overstated, and organisations that get it right now will be far ahead of their competition.

Finally, we'll give you a quick tour of motivational psychology, the 'engine' that drives each and every one of us to act the way we do, and the thing that gamification targets specifically. These drives are common to all of us, but the exact way they push us to act will vary based on the individual and the situation they are faced with. This is important to understand, as you will be basing your gamification solution on these levers. Get it wrong, and you'll build something that your customers won't engage with or care about.

So as you can see, Section 1 is the – bluntly titled – theory part of the book, but don't let that put you off even if you are familiar with a lot of the concepts we'll be covering. Understanding what gamification is and the psychological levers that link with it will help you to build something that truly engages with your customers, something that most gamification solutions fail to do.

CHAPTER ONE

What is gamification?

Let's start at the very beginning. What is gamification?

Unfortunately, defining gamification is tricky, because at the moment there isn't one single definition that everyone agrees on – even though it's been used across different industries and professions for several years now.

There are multiple streams of thought (and arguments) on what gamification is from academics, professionals, consultants and 'gurus', but while many agree with each other, they can disagree on some pretty fundamental things.

So to better explain gamification to you, we've picked out a handful of experts with whom we mostly agree, and we'll work through their theories to give you a better idea on the current thinking on gamification. Note, though, that while there are many more thought leaders out there who we could have listed, we've chosen who we have because they represent a cross-section of the most popular and relevant definitions. It is from these explanations of gamification that we'll then explain our own working definition which we'll be using throughout this book.

It's important to understand and agree on these basic terms and ideas now before we move on to more complex concepts. Otherwise, it becomes too easy to get lost or to misunderstand points later on in the book. That said, more experienced readers may choose to skip this section and move on to the practical sections of the book.

Asking the experts: 'What is gamification?'

The Consultant

Yu-Kai Chou is an author and active consultant on gamification and the wider application of these principles, which he calls *'behavioural design'*. He is the creator of the Octalysis Framework[1] (a method for quantifying the impacts of gamification on different psychological motivators), and the author of *Actionable Gamification: Beyond Points, Badges, and Leaderboards*[2]. He is a large influence on our thinking when it comes to general gamification, and we highly recommend you read his book and online articles.

Yu-Kai Chou believes that:

'Gamification is the craft of deriving all the fun and addicting elements found in games and applying them to real-world or productive activities. This is what I call "Human-Focused Design" as opposed to the "Function-Focused Design." It is a design process that optimises for the human in the system, as opposed to pure efficiency of the system.'[3]

Yu-Kai Chou's emphasis is on designing a system for the human end-user using the fun and addictive parts of games. Hopefully, you can already see how this type of thinking fits perfectly with the customer-focused marketing strategies that you will no doubt be trying to deploy in your organisation.

Like us, Yu-Kai Chou focuses heavily on human psychology and designing gamification in ways that appeal to specific motivators of players. We cover motivational psychology in later chapters, as this will be key to understanding why gamification is so effective, and how you can best deploy it for your specific customer base, industry and organisation.

The Analyst

Brian Burke is a Research Vice President at Gartner and author of the book *Gamify: How Gamification Motivates People to Do Extraordinary Things*[4]. In his book, Burke discusses the origins of the term gamification and how such an 'ugly word' has maintained its grasp on the industry despite numerous (unsuccessful) attempts to change it over the years (like Chou's 'behavioural design' that we mentioned).

Unsurprisingly given his background, he uses Gartner's definition of gamification:

> *'The use of game mechanics and experience design to digitally engage and motivate people to achieve their goals.'*[5]

Burke highlights the use of game mechanics and experience design to influence motivation. He does seem to imply that gamification is purely a digital application; however, this is something that we disagree with as it can be equally effective (and sometimes more feasible for small businesses) when done non-digitally.

What Burke does point out, though, is that gamification is about motivating people to achieve their goals. 'Their goals' is vital here, too many marketers have failed because they forgot this fundamental principle. When you try to gamify something, you need to remember to focus on the player – not yourself.

This book aims to show you many examples of game mechanics and how you can meaningfully apply them to your marketing both online and offline to help your players achieve their goals. We want you to be able to use these techniques regardless of whether you are a start-up with no marketing budget or part of a mega-corporation with limitless resources.

The Professor

Kevin Werbach is an associate professor of legal studies and business ethics at The Wharton School at the University of Pennsylvania. He is the creator and instructor of the Gamification MOOC on Coursera, and co-author of *For the Win: How Game Thinking Can Revolutionize Your Business*[6].

Werbach's commonly cited definition of gamification is one of the more widely spread academic ones, covering many of the different aspects of games, game design and gamification itself:

> *'Gamification is the use of game elements and game design techniques in non-game contexts.'*[7]

Now this definition may throw up more questions than answers depending on your pre-existing knowledge. What are game elements? What exactly is game design? What are non-game contexts?

The answers to these questions are vital building blocks to understanding what gamification is, which is why we've decided to take apart Kevin Werbach's definition: *'Gamification is the use of game elements and game design techniques in non-game contexts'*, and explain it piece by piece.

We'll use these answers to then put together our own gamification definition – that is specifically for marketing gamification – that we'll be using for the rest of the book.

Before we begin: What is a game?

Many of you, depending on your demographic, hobbies and tech knowledge, may have dismissed this question and just labelled games as computer games, card games or sports games. Moreover, you'd be halfway to the correct answer, but what *actually* makes them games?

It's important to agree on what a game is before we jump into Werbach's definition fully. That way you'll know whether you've made a game, or just another shallow corporate attempt to make something 'fun'.

Bernard Suits, author of *The Grasshopper: Games, Life and Utopia*[8], focused his work on what games are and how they impact us and our whole society. He made meaningful efforts to define what a game is, and came up with the following rules for defining if something is a game:

Rule 1: All games must have a pre-defined end goal for the players

In hide-and-seek, the hider's pre-defined goal is to remain hidden for as long as possible, while the seeker's pre-defined goal is to find the hider as fast as possible. You can see how having goals in a game is important. Without them, nobody would know what to do, and there would be chaos and little motivation. With them, each player understands what they need to achieve, and this is the primary motivator for why players act the way they do while in the game.

Rule 2: All games must have a set of limitations that determine how the players can act

Continuing our hide-and-seek example, the hider usually agrees on a set area in which they can hide (like the playground), while the seeker agrees that they will close their eyes for a set amount of time while the hider hides – so no peeking!

These limitations/rules are vital for games to be successful. By imposing structure through these rules, ordinary tasks and actions can become challenging and even fun to perform. Imagine how boring hide-and-seek would be if you watched where the hider hid. Many businesses neglect this aspect of games by trying to make their gamified processes as easy as possible with no limitations, taking away a fundamental element of the game itself and destroying the player's motivation to play and be creative.

Rule 3: All players will adopt a 'lusory' attitude

A lusory attitude is a mindset where you are playing a game and voluntarily follow that game's rules. Players must care about and invest in the game for the game's own sake and adopt a fair-play or sportsman-like behaviour towards other players and the game itself.

In our hide-and-seek example, there are no real physical boundaries in the game, but all the players inherently accept that a certain area is where the game is played, and outside of that area the game no longer exists (so no hiding in the classrooms or running out of the school grounds!).

A lusory attitude is vital when applying gamification to real life; without it, your players will not engage with your game as a game and will instead try to cheat the system. Alternatively, they will not recognise where the game begins and ends, causing unintended behaviours in other areas of your business.

Rule 4: All players must voluntarily play the game

One thing that Suits does not include in his three rules, but does mention in his definition of what a game is, is that all players must take part of their own free will. This is technically a part of a lusory attitude, but it is important enough that we have designated it as a separate rule.

If a player is forced to play, then it's not a game. This is often a failure in many gamified systems as businesses force their customers and employees to engage with a game and are left scratching their heads over the lack of engagement. For example, many people's first encounter with gamification usually comes from HR's attempts at making mandatory health and safety training 'fun'.

Warning: When a game isn't a game

But do all these things need to be present for a game to be a game? You may be thinking that as a child, you can't remember ever adopting a 'lusory attitude' consciously, and don't recall ever stating goals and rules for every game you played. The likely answer is that you did these things automatically and unconsciously, with little mental effort.

However, there is also a chance that you weren't actually playing a game at all, you might have just been playing.

'Play' is unstructured fun with no pre-determined end goal or purpose. Some good examples of 'play' are children playing pretend, or free-drawing from their imaginations. 'Play' is fun and engaging for those playing, but as you can see it has little use in motivating the players towards a specific goal, making it ineffective when trying to gamify a process and motivate end users.

It is this structure (or lack of it) that makes the difference between games and 'play'. The lower you are on the sliding scale of structure, the further you get from traditional games and their goal orientation. However, the further you slide towards more structure, the more restrictive the game becomes until there is no 'play' left.

You need to carefully engineer your gamified process to find the sweet-spot of structure that lets your players engage with your game efficiently – giving your players goals and motivation, but not having such a lack of play that it is no longer fun. This can usually only be found through extensive (play-)testing of your concept.

So, is this all there is to a game? A set of goals, rules to create structure, and the right player mindset?

Legendary game designer Sid Meier said: '*A good game is a series of interesting choices*'[9]. Meier highlights the fact that games can be good or bad, and that the distinction between the two can often depend on what he refers to as 'interesting choices'. These interesting choices are fundamentally linked to the game's structure but are further enhanced by how the game has been designed and the game elements that it is built from.

But now we're back to our original set of questions: what are game elements and design? Let's return to Werbach's gamification definition and our breakdown of each of the terms within it.

What are game elements?

'Gamification is the use of game elements and game design techniques in non-game contexts.'

So now we know what a game is, but how do you put one together? You've got a set of rules and an overall objective for the players, so what comes next?

Let's look at football (or soccer for some) as an example. With our definition of a game, we have 22 voluntary players split into two teams, who understand and agree to the rules of football, who have a defined area to play in, and who all have the overall objective of winning the game by scoring more goals than the other team. Sounds great, but we are forgetting something; how can they play without a ball?

When building a game, or more specifically in our case, a gamified process or product, you need to include these 'things' that the player interacts with or references when they are playing. These 'things' are what we call 'game elements' and are the building blocks of all games.

To continue our football example, the game elements we could list are:

- The football itself
- The goal posts
- Points when a team scores a goal (one goal equals one point)
- A countdown timer for the game's length
- Leaderboards if the results of the game are recorded against other games over time

And so on...

But rather than list every game element now, what's important to understand at this stage is that game elements are the individual parts of the game. The building blocks that allow you to play. Together with game design, they make the game, but by themselves they do nothing.

Too often businesses will just cherry-pick individual game elements, like achievements and leaderboards, and try to stick them on to a process they intend to gamify without any thought to game design and the player experience. This often results in confused and unmotivated players, often leading to unintended side effects and behaviours.

A good example of these unintended side effects was Disney's gamified housekeeping scheme[10].

Disney used points and a leaderboard to rank staff on how many rooms were serviced and how often laundry was done – with the lowest scoring team member being reprimanded (or sometimes fired). This initially led to a huge spike in productivity in the short term (good), but it also led to numerous complaints about half-tidied rooms, damaged linen and poor employee morale (bad). They hadn't thought about the player experience.

It's also not about the sheer number of game elements you can think up and apply to a situation; you need to think about how these game elements interact with each other, the game itself, and the players.

This strategy of how you merge game elements and bind them with your game structure is called game design, although it will only be successful if it motivates players to do the desired actions.

What is game design?

'Gamification is the use of game elements and game design techniques in non-game contexts.'

Games are more than just a pile of game elements. If you just dump game elements on to a structure with no thought, you'll likely have a disaster. This is where game design comes in.

Game design is how you take your collection of specific and relevant game elements and put them together within the game's set rules and structure to motivate your players towards an end goal. This requires you to understand what your game is, what you want your players to do in certain situations, and what game elements are available to you.

Don't worry if you don't know this yet; we'll guide you through it later. But you will need to understand:

Why are you creating this game and why should someone play it?

Games are designed for an end purpose – often for fun and to challenge the player – but in marketing gamification that purpose should be a business-oriented goal like customer engagement, conversion rates and retention. You need to approach and align the game's purpose from two angles – your business goals and your customer's goals – if you want to implement gamification effectively. We will go into much more detail on setting appropriate goals in Chapter 15.

Who is the game for?

You need to understand that successful games are focused on the player, not the game designer or the company they work for. Game designers understand that the player needs to be the centre of the game and feel that the game is for them. This player focus lends itself well to customer-focused marketing, and we will explore more on how to segment your customer base and understand their motivations and gamer behaviour in Chapter 14.

How will the above change over time?

Games and their players will change over the course of your game. Every player starts off uninitiated and will require onboarding with tutorials and instructions. As time goes on these players will (hopefully) require fewer instructions but will become bored with repeating the same mechanics and will start looking for greater challenges and new experiences. Your most experienced players will have seen everything your game has to offer; what will you do to keep them around to help the latest batch of novices? Every game needs to take changing player needs into consideration; in Chapter 16 we will show you how to map out your player's journey and keep them engaged every step of the way.

How will my game look?

Finally, it would be best if you considered how the players experience the game. This is the overall look and feel of the endgame and should be linked to your brand if you want to ensure players can associate your business with the gamified product/process they are interacting with. The game's aesthetics is what most people associate with game design. This is important to get right as the final quality and brand cohesion must be high to encourage players to take part, as if there is any disconnect from your brand's identity or the player's expectation then they will quickly abandon the game. Remember, your goal is not to make the next AAA blockbuster computer game, but to create a visually cohesive experience that fits your brand promise.

What are non-game contexts?

'Gamification is the use of game elements and game design techniques in non-game contexts.'

This is the core of what gamification actually is. If you just build a game that doesn't impact your business, then congratulations, you've built a game, but you haven't implemented gamification to improve your business. To practise gamification, your 'game' must integrate into your business (the non-game context) and align with your business goals.

This book is focused on marketing gamification specifically, so when we talk about gamifying non-game contexts, we are talking about use cases like:

- Gamifying your company website to encourage customers to complete their profiles fully like LinkedIn, who used progress bars and tutorials to guide customers through profile best practices to ensure they reach 100 per cent completion of their profiles.[11]
- Gamifying your product trial to increase conversion rates to the full product like Autodesk, who built a series of quests into their product trial to encourage players to take on more and more difficult challenges using the company's software suite.[12]
- Gamifying your customer service desk to improve customer satisfaction scores or drive down response times like FreshDesk, who used a combination of points, levels and awards to engage with customer service employees to respond quickly and accurately to help requests.[13]

Non-game contexts can also either be externally or internally focused.

- Externally-focused solutions will impact your customer directly, and you should try and align your business goals with your customer's goals to increase engagement.
- Internally-focused solutions will impact your own business and employees and can cover multiple teams who share the same goals.

Traditionally, external gamification is associated with marketing as it is focused on improving customer engagement, while internal gamification is usually the realm of HR, Finance, IT and Operations (often linked to improving learning, helpdesks, compliance, etc.).

However, as the scope of marketing increases, you will find that internal gamification has applications in customer service, internal marketing, sales and team management.

The easiest way to ensure you aren't failing at this when you've reached this hurdle is to ask yourself: Do I have a business-relevant and measurable goal? Does the gamified process I've designed contribute towards that goal? And for extra credit, does my business goal align in some way with my player's end goals? More on this in Section 3.

What isn't gamification?

Let's look at the reverse side of the coin now – how do you know when gamification has failed? By knowing what gamification isn't, you should be better prepared to create a successful gamification solution. It is a tricky question, but now is a good time to talk about some of the pitfalls many businesses fall into when trying to implement gamification properly.

Using only game elements without game design

Declaring that your customer has earned 10 points for clicking a button, or has earned an achievement for posting their first comment, are examples of applying game elements, but if you have not tied these elements together with thoughtful game design then you do not have successful gamification, but rather a hollow experience.

One example of this pitfall was Google, who implemented a badge system into their newsreader.[14]

Whenever you read news articles through this Google system it would record what you were reading and periodically award you with badges based on your interests; the problem was that nobody else could see these badges and most people who earned them were unaware that they had them. A result of this was that players would receive titles like 'sports buff' after reading five sports-related articles, and would complain that the achievements had no meaning or significance to them.

Just a game without a non-game context

If you create a game that doesn't link to your business objectives then, as we've said, you have created a game, but you have not implemented gamification (look on the bright side though, your company now has a game, and you're now technically a game developer). To avoid this pitfall, you need to identify what the metrics are that you are trying to influence, and actively design a game that will impact them.

A game that nobody wants to play

While you can create a gamified product/service, it needs to have a (good) reason to be played. That reason can be for fun, challenge or reward, but you need to have a game that people will want to play.

And how can you know this? Data.

Are people already doing what you want them to do, but your gamification will make it easier? How do people find your game? Are they abandoning it or are they coming back again and again?

It's this kind of testing that could have saved Marriott a lot of money when it developed its recruitment game 'MyMarriottHotel'[15], a Farmville clone that was intended to teach players what it's like to work at a Marriott hotel. The problem was that the game wasn't very interesting, with simple click-and-forget quests that had no real relation to the game's objectives of showing the player what life was like working for Marriott, and no real reason for players to play the game as it didn't connect to the player's chances of getting an interview or proving their skills. This led to players abandoning the game quickly after realising this fact.

Finally, what is gamification then?

We've briefly examined what some of the current thinkers define gamification as, and then specifically unpacked Kevin Werbach's definition – examining each part of his definition to look at the meanings of games, game elements, game design and non-game contexts.

A lot of these definitions largely agree on the broad strokes of what gamification is, and we aren't interested in the academic arguments that make up the nitty-gritty of what for example is and isn't a game element – we're talking about practical applications here.

But a definition is important, it is how you will know for certain whether what you create is actually gamification or not – and it's a measure you can use to make sure you haven't fallen into one of the pitfalls we have discussed so far by accidentally creating something that is actually a game, or worse, just a mess.

We've looked at the definitions provided by prominent thinkers in the space; the consultant, the analyst and the professor. But what's missing? If you're like us, you're probably scratching your head at the lack of input from business owners and marketers within organisations.

The fact is that most of the noise in the gamification space comes from some thought leaders arguing over semantics and some consultants who are trying to sell their services by 'bigging up' gamification's benefits. There are still too few inside practitioners in gamification who are publicly talking about this stuff. They are usually too busy acting on it.

This is one of the main reasons we felt so compelled to write this book. We have both worked with gamification inside real companies and feel that gamification can really help many organisations to build compelling experiences for their customers – they just need to apply a no-bullsh*t marketing gamification model to get there.

So, what is our definition? We define marketing gamification as:

'Marketing Gamification is the thoughtful application of relevant game elements to solve real-life customer problems that are connected to your organisation.'

Note several keywords in our definition:

- **Thoughtful application**: This is our nod to game design; you should not just dump game elements on to a system or process and think you're done. Every decision must be made for a reason. Always be asking WHY.
- **Relevant game elements**: Less can be more, every game element you include should be there for a good reason and should add to the player experience in some way. Don't just add something because you can, or your boss told you to or because your competitors have.
- **Real-life customer problems**: Always make sure that your gamification solution is impacting the real world, that it is solving your customers' real problems/needs in a tangible, measurable way. If you can't measure it, then it doesn't exist.
- **Connected to your organisation**: Congratulations, you've built a gamification solution that solves your customers' dental hygiene problems, but your company sells cars.... While it's important to design your gamification for customer problems, make sure these connect to your organisation's goals!

So, write it down, tattoo it on your marketing executives, and put it at the top of every document you have about your gamification project. This should be the mantra you remember from this book, it is how you should judge every gamification solution you come across – and it is how we will judge yours!

Summary: Chapter 1

Gamification is a broad term used across multiple industries and professions. There are many different definitions, but many share similar characteristics. Chiefly that they are all based on games and use elements from games to motivate people; these elements are tied together with game design (a method of thinking about how players will react to a given game); and are all designed to impact real-life situations in some way, motivating real people to take specific actions that should benefit a business or process.

We also learned that all games should consist of four rules:

- Rule 1: All games have a pre-defined end goal for the players.
- Rule 2: All games have a set of limitations that determine how the players can act.
- Rule 3: All players will adopt a lusory attitude.
- Rule 4: All players must voluntarily play the game.

And finally, remember our own definition: **Marketing Gamification is the thoughtful application of relevant game elements to solve real-life customer problems that are connected to your organisation.**

Next steps:

- Write down our definition somewhere and keep it visible: Marketing Gamification is the thoughtful application of relevant game elements to solve real-life customer problems that are connected to your organisation.
- Think about your favourite game, whether it's a computer game, a board game or a sport. List that game's game elements and think about how the game has been designed to motivate its players to achieve certain goals. Are some game elements more effective than others? Why?
- Now you know more about what gamification is, can you think of three examples where you have been impacted by or experienced gamification? Were they successful? Or immediately noticeable?

CHAPTER TWO

The rise of games

You (hopefully) picked up this book looking for new ways to grow your business – but you may be sceptical about gamification and how games can improve your marketing. We understand the scepticism (we were sceptics too), so we've dedicated this and the following chapter to showing you why games and gamification are important, where they came from, and how they can impact your marketing strategies.

But why should you care? On the surface, the most important reason for gamifying your business is that gamification can have a very real impact on marketing and people. It offers you tools and methods to:

1) Motivate your customers to act in a certain way (share blog posts on social media, visit specific stores at certain times, register products on your website, fill in forms, etc.).
2) Build brand awareness and loyalty, and
3) Incentivise new and existing customers to use, buy and talk about your products/services.

One example of gamification's impact on marketing is the popular chocolate brand M&M's, who managed to achieve all of the above with their 'Eye-Spy Pretzel' campaign to launch pretzel-flavoured candy in the US.[16]

It was an ingenious and inexpensive strategy where they used the game eye-spy, and a type of 'Where's Wally/Waldo' finding game on their Facebook page. Followers and customers were challenged with a 'scavenger-hunt' mechanic to find the little pretzel guy hidden among the candy in various picture graphics. It was a huge success in the US as many people liked and shared it, allowing it to go viral, expanding the game's audience and increasing brand awareness of the whole brand and (specifically through the game) their latest product launch into pretzels.

This worked for them as the gamification was inexpensive to create and run, was simple for customers to understand and play, was fun and engaging, and wasn't directly linked to anything commercial (although it did help sell more of the product in the long run).

This is only a minor example of a company that incorporated a game into their social media product launch marketing, but this book will give you many more ideas, tools and techniques to incorporate gamification into every aspect of your marketing strategy.

Gamification can be powerful when done right. But where does this power come from? What makes games so effective in the first place?

The dawn of games

To better understand gamification, you should know where games come from and where they are going.

Games have always been a part of human society, with some of the oldest games dating back to over 5,000 years ago in what is now the Middle East and the areas around the Mediterranean Sea. These were not complex games by our modern standards, but they had rules, goals and they brought people together.

Games and playing together, according to Johan Huizinga, is really what helped create a human cultural society and all its complexities: '[Play] is older than culture, for culture, however inadequately defined, always presupposes human society, and animals have not waited for the man to teach them their playing.'[17]

Playing in this sense, then, is where everything started; art, philosophy, war, language and so on. And by that extension playing and games occurred organically as a means of exploring these concepts.

We can see this relationship between games imitating life in some of the first games created. Games that we know today such as Chess, Go or Checkers are competitive zero-sum games that are essentially depictions of a battle. While games that involved chance with dice, which have surprise and mystery woven in, are the grass roots of modern gambling games.[18]

But what do these games have in common?

As we've discussed, games need players, rules, limitations and a goal. It's these elements that suck players in, the structure of the game that makes achieving the goal difficult, but not impossible.

From around the 15th Century, structures and rules really began to take shape and define what gaming is, giving them an air of professionalism. For many centuries being able to play games such as chess, or checkers or card games, at a 'professional' level, was the purview of the elite – those that had the opportunity to dedicate their own time to learn the craft of the game.

An outcome of this pursuit of professionalism is that games gained popularity and became more widespread as society allowed its citizens to have more leisure time. People had more time to play games, and spend more time watching others play them. One example of the broader adoption and democratisation of professional gaming is with the first televised championships of sport and chess in the 20th Century, which quickly expanded to televised game shows, and now with the Internet: video game streamers.

Live-action televised gaming, along with miniature tabletop, role-play (war-)gaming, can be a strong argument for the eventual step into electronic and computer gaming, which is now one of the largest industries in the world. But more importantly, with gaming and the rise of electronics and the digital world, the democratisation of enjoyment, coupled with challenge and learning has spread even further. And with mobile gaming, the old belief that gaming is for the elite has been entirely removed.

Regardless of age, gender or culture, every single person can enjoy gaming, and reap the benefits from it, as we have done for generations, and will do so for generations to come.

The changing landscape of games and gamers

Millennials and the generations to come will all most likely grow up with games being one of their central forms of entertainment. As everyone is becoming more connected, technology is becoming cheaper, and companies are getting increasingly better at learning and customising, games will be interwoven into the very fabric of our everyday lives.

But are games just for entertainment?

As we know from various studies, games remain fun even when they request exceptional effort from us, and that is why many educational systems are gamifying to better retain learner attention and intellectual investment.

As James Paul Gee, Professor of Literary Studies at Arizona State University has noted, games force individuals to learn quickly and adapt to their own unique sets of rules and challenges, and games do certainly ask people to put in the time and energy regardless of the expected difficulty.[19]

So, if games are asking this of children in and outside of schools as they grow up, then they will invariably be expecting a similar environment when they enter the workforce. And you can expect the same thing when they become fully-fledged consumers in their own right.

This expectation of generations now and to come is why gamification is of such importance. The gamer generation isn't about to come; it's here now. These players are often the ones in search of deeper meaning and more immersive experiences. And if you're not offering this, they will find it somewhere else.

Let's go through some statistics that illustrate who these players are[20]:

- As of 2018 worldwide, there are approximately 2.3 billion gamers who actively and regularly play video games or use social games, with over half of these coming from the Asia-Pacific region. This doesn't even count the number of people playing card and board games.
- While gaming is often associated with younger people, approximately 15 per cent of gamers worldwide are aged between 51 and 65. Not only that, but 63 per cent of all gamers in 2018 were 21 to 50 years of age. These numbers clearly show that video games are played much more frequently by adults.
- The number of hours spent on gaming on and offline is between four and eight hours per week. These hours can be on video games, but also on traditional board games and the like.
- At least 40 per cent of those people play with someone they know. And unsurprisingly 50 per cent of gamers are those that play social games. These social games can be multiplayer games like *Call of Duty* but are just as likely to be games on social media or apps with multiplayer features.
- The next question is always then, how many men and how many women play these games? Well, the split is becoming narrower every day. Currently, we're looking at a 54 per cent male and 46 per cent female split. But that's a rough average across all ages. If you start looking at specific age ranges then the split will either move more in favour of women or more in favour of men. And then we haven't even touched upon specific nations and cultures to evaluate their male–female splits.

These numbers may or may not come as a shock depending on your background, but what will probably come as a surprise to you is the money that's behind those numbers.

In 2018 the top earners in video-game revenue across the world were China with 37.9 billion USD and the US with 30.4 billion USD.

Eurasia and Africa account for 28.7 billion USD. And the Asia-Pacific region as a whole has 71.4 billion USD in revenue.[21]

The biggest upcoming business and spender in gaming currently is eSports. eSports is the catch-all moniker for all digital games that can be played at a professional competitive level. These games involve athletes, much like traditional sports, only their field of play is in the virtual world.

The amounts involved in eSports are staggering. The global revenue for eSports in 2018 was at 865 million USD, and is expected to rise to 1.8 billion USD by 2022[22]. 2018 saw 737 individual eSports events, with sponsorships at 456.7 million USD, advertising at 189.2 million USD and merchandise and ticket sales at 103.7 million USD[23].

These are all huge numbers, and as the age ranges increase alongside the formats and adoption of games, these numbers will only keep increasing. While we're not suggesting you get involved in eSports or try to turn your business into one, we are demonstrating how prevalent gaming has become in our society and how it is only growing in popularity and changing the expectations of your staff and customers.

But how does this growth in gaming translate into gamification?

In 2016, the expectation was that the gamification industry will grow to 12 billion USD by 2021 and to 19 billion USD by 2023. Much of this growth is centred around gamified digital tools for learning institutions and the HR and L&D sector, specifically on training for healthcare, health & safety and compliance training[24]. This is where most of the publicity for gamification as we know it is.

But what about marketing gamification?

We know from our own research that gamification has been growing in size year after year, and while everyone is shouting about gamification learning, the real successes as we will show you are in gamification marketing[25].

Marketing flirted with gamification a few years ago and quickly announced it was a fad after thousands of businesses tried and failed to implement it as a get-rich-quick scheme. It was this quick-fix mentality and a lack of any real structure or guidebook for marketers to follow that doomed gamification to fail.

But did it really fail? We'll show you in multiple examples and case studies in this book that gamification never died. Many large companies kept doing it but didn't make a lot of noise or call it gamification. A silent revolution has been taking place, and this book will show you how to take the fruits of this revolution and apply them to your own marketing.

Summary: Chapter 2

Games have always been pervasive in human society worldwide, and now in the 21st Century, it is becoming a mainstream activity across all ages, genders and cultures. This spread, combined with the rise of the Internet and eSports has rocketed the gaming economy to rival and exceed movies, board games and some popular sports. Games are here to stay and are becoming more and more integrated into everyday life; marketers who wait to implement gamification will soon be behind the curve.

Next steps:

- Immerse yourself in games online or offline, and learn what makes them appealing and what about them appeals to you.
- As you move through the book, keep in mind what you are trying to gamify and start looking into what technological tools can help you to achieve this.
- As you make a list of tools, include analogue ones as well; having a list will help you to understand what is both financially and practically viable for your marketing gamification.

CHAPTER THREE

The power behind games

Control, structure and escapism

As we've seen, games have not only become popular and big business but are now a part of everyone's everyday life. This is despite the stereotypical, negative image of a 'gamer' that formed around video games in recent years and which is thankfully being dispelled as gaming becomes more mainstream.

Games are not just video games; they cover the broad range of all games that we all play. Games have always been important, but it is only recently that they have become big business and pervasive across so many demographics. But is gaming a recent phenomenon?

Jane McGonigal in her book *Reality is Broken* (2011) uses the example of the Lydian civilisation of Asia Minor in the Ancient World, and how this civilisation survived drought and famine with the use and help of collectively played games: '*Games made life bearable. Games gave a starving population a feeling of power in a powerless situation, a sense of structure in a chaotic environment.*'[26]

The keywords here are a sense of power or rather 'empowerment' and 'structure'.

For many, modern society is very chaotic and having systems in place like games can provide a much-needed alternative 'escape-valve' that offers structure and empowerment where there is none. This is obvious from McGonigal's example of the Lydians, who were able to survive famine by diverting their attention through the use of games which were unrelated to their current circumstances. Don't mistake this as them ignoring their problems, but rather dealing with a situation they were powerless to solve, by using the structures and power given to them by games to keep control of some aspect of their lives.

This need for structured comprehension is why we're attracted to (visual and interactive) mediums of entertainment; they offer us an alternative to a reality we don't want to, or can't, control or are unable to deal with at that moment. Fiction in film was the first instance in the modern age that gave us a sense of vicarious control; we empathise with the protagonists who appear to understand their lot in life and are in charge of their destiny.

The next natural step for structure, escapism and control was then towards the gaming world. A world with clear rules and goals. Here the player understands everything and has everything under control, or at least they have the illusion of understanding and control. That is why games are so appealing, being both visual and a form of cognitive interaction to help better deal with 'dire' situations.

Knowledge as an immersive hook

Beyond the eye-candy of visual games, the most attractive aspect of creating games or gamifying experiences is for their ability to effectively transfer knowledge and ideas, from your business to your consumer.

Making your experiences more game-like should make them more engaging and immersive for your customers, or rather your players as that is what they are now.

The experience becomes more engaging because, as those who are familiar with games – especially online games – know, that information should be readily available and should be received 'just-in-time'. Just-in-time refers to acquiring knowledge exactly when it's relevant and applicable. And in a world of mobile connectivity, all information is on-demand and accessible everywhere.

The process of gamification offers a framework where engaging, fun, on-demand and just-in-time informative experiences can be created anywhere for anyone. And that is the crux of why it is important for you because you are creating informative experiences for your players. People no longer wish to be fed; they want to interact and to be part of the (brand) story you are developing for them. And people love that because they can participate and become smarter because of it.

Community and self-empowerment for your customers

When you create a community around your product through your campaign, your players will want to do more with – and for – that community, they'll want to interact with the other players involved. This is a type of collective self-empowerment that hopefully grows organically within your gamification campaign. In Chapter 11 we will explore community and belonging a bit further.

Playboy isn't really an example of a company you'd think of straight away when talking about gamified platforms and collective self-empowerment. They already have a product that everyone intrinsically wants: sex. But despite that, they wanted to target younger and newer subscribers to their brand. They, therefore, partnered with Bunchball, a web gamification company to create a Facebook-like app called Miss Social[27].

As the name suggests, it created a social environment for new users to engage with what could be called a crowdsourced, community-led version of *Playboy* magazine. Women who aspired to be in *Playboy* could upload photos and try to win votes so that they could be featured on Playboy.com. The system worked by giving users votes over a time period. Users could then save up those votes and use them all or partly on various days to vote for their favourite featured individual(s).

The women who wanted to win could engage their friends or engage with the community in general through this social platform and gain more votes. As they were delivering the product – photos – they were creating an organic community around the app and themselves by delivering content that people wanted and would vote for.

This social, community-based gamification project was pretty successful for Playboy, as they had an 85 per cent rate of re-engagement with their brand and a 60 per cent increase in revenues per month. It would seem that in today's age, basic desires like sex aren't enough to engage; there needs to be meaning and a sense of working together as a community to get people to commit to your brand.

These examples of communities working together, and people being empowered to harness the power of a community, are some of the strongest aspects that you can gain when using a well-implemented gamification marketing campaign. Another activity in life that you would traditionally think doesn't need much help to become more fun or engaging is sport and health & wellbeing. But Nike also felt it could use the power of gamification to improve just that.

Thus, another great example of where a community's members helped each other to improve is with Nike and their Nike+ Fuelband accessory.

Nike had launched this particular product of theirs, the Nike+ Fuelband, back in 2012, and since then we've come to know Nike as a company that takes an apparent active interest in the health and wellbeing of its customers.

What the Fuelband does is measure and monitor the user's movements. To keep track of these measurements the user would need to download a Nike+ app. Through this they can check their workouts done, calories burned and so on.

The initial thing to note with the app and the Fuelband is that the players are receiving instant feedback on how they are doing. This is part of that on-demand and just-in-time feedback mechanic that invests players' attention into a system they are using. As each player can see how they did yesterday, versus how they are doing today, they can accordingly change their exercise regime to achieve their own optimum workout efficiency for tomorrow.

The second thing to note is that Nike released the Fuelband via their Nike+ Community. This allowed the various players to compete with each other. Each member of the community could share and compare their own achievements versus friends or versus the best in the community, as all achievements are visible via a community leaderboard.

Additionally, as each player went through the Fuelband app, they would slowly unlock features and gain badges for what they had achieved, thus promoting a return to the app to see what else they can achieve.

This campaign from Nike was very successful, and it organically created brand loyalty, as each player wants to be fit and healthy, but also wants to be part of a community that shares these values, and the added game elements of competition and achievements helped facilitate this. This success demonstrates that many associate healthy living with the Nike brand and the mechanics used in the Fuelband are now also ubiquitous in every fitness app.

Communities and communal narratives for your brand

Wanting to be part of a community and part of its journey is a great marketing tool. Customers enjoy being with like-minded individuals, especially if they are the ones in-the-know and they were the ones that purchased the correct products, your products.

Another example of where this kind of community gamification is used is Samsung's 'Samsung Nation'. Samsung Nation, as the name suggests, aims to create a community around the Samsung customer base and use it to drive customer engagement. Within the community, users can review Samsung products, participate in discussions, watch videos and so on. Each time they contributed to the community they would progress through levels, earning badges and achievements.

This is clearly a basic gamified example, as it simply uses some low-level game elements such as badges and achievements to help increase a sense of brand loyalty. The real purpose behind it, though, was to increase product reviews for Samsung, and it achieved this. Samsung saw an increase of 500 per cent in their product reviews. So, in a sense it was highly successful; the community felt great about what they had to say. Whether it expanded the community with new customers is possible, but the purpose was to increase brand loyalty and communal homogeneity in the already present customer base.

Admittedly this is only a surface level example of brand loyalty and community building in a marketing gamification example. In the short term, the company saw an increase in reviews and people/customers would see these amazing reviews, but as time passed people would become wary of an older review.

If you want to make an experience enjoyable and engaging in the long term, you will need something more than that, and that something more is a 'narrative'. The narrative for a business is its brand and its corporate motivation. A narrative alone, though, only offers a part of what players are looking for. It may only be unconscious for some, but the majority of players want a communal experience that's challenging and offers meaningful learning from the 'narrative'.

A great example of a company creating immersive story worlds to promote its brand is Autodesk. Autodesk took the idea of narrative creation and customisation and targeted it to a specific user base. If you're unfamiliar with Autodesk, they are a 3D modelling software company, commonly used in the film and game industries.

Autodesk took their traditional trial software and gamified it. Trials have always been a function-focused aspect of any software sale. It's there to give the consumer a taste of what the software can do and based upon that they will hopefully buy it. Autodesk, however, decided that they would create a custom player journey for their target audience in the trial.

During the trial period for their 3D modelling software, the player would be taken through a tutorial named the 'Undiscovered Territory'. The tutorial would show them how to use the various elements in the software to go from a digital sketch to a fully textured 3D asset. As you can tell by the name, the player is taken through a narrative of discovering various hidden cities and undiscovered territories. This meant there was an added meaning to the trial, you weren't just there to randomly click options, but you were part of a journey of discovery, with a clear goal and challenges you needed to overcome.

This gamified trial was a huge success for Autodesk; their trial usage increased by 54 per cent, the buy clicks increased by 15 per cent and the channel revenue per trial increased by 29 per cent. All of that is a pretty positive reason as to why gamification can be useful.

What can be seen from the above examples in gamification is that the right gamification processes are about creating good, efficient and well-structured environments. Your players need to be able to quickly access, understand and easily use your product or service. Beyond that, they will need other pieces such as a 'narrative', but also the freedom of choice in whether to engage in your product or service and also instant and useful feedback mechanics.

Summary: Chapter 3

The power of games and gamification is that they allow you to add a system that contains a clear structure with goals, challenges, outcomes and consequences that are easily understood and grasped by your players. Allowing your players to learn about your brand and product while learning new skills for the game is a way to get them effectively invested. And to keep them invested, you need to ensure that a community organically grows around your gamified experience, as well as having an engaging brand narrative.

Next steps:

- Think about what experiences, games or otherwise had a structured system that engaged you and allowed you to feel in control.
- Consider what communities you are part of: book clubs, gym clubs, hobby clubs. What is it about them that appeals to you and how do they maintain your continued investment in them?
- Take your brand and see what stories exist about it, ones that you and your colleagues have about it and stories that your customers have about it, good or bad.

CHAPTER FOUR

The biology of motivation

Do you feel in control, or do you sometimes feel an urge to act in a certain way? We are not talking about extremes like gambling or substance addiction, but everyday flaws like your desire to have one more piece of chocolate or to finish that next level of *Candy Crush*.

The question is: why do you do what you do?

Most of us act the way we do because we expect that by acting in a certain way, we'll feel good (or feel less bad) – although usually in the short term. We eat an extra piece of chocolate because our mouth drools with the anticipation of eating it, or we play another level of a video game because we know we'll feel good if we complete it.

Sure, we can override this short-term thinking and stick to a diet or focus on getting our work done – but it's always a conscious effort to steer ourselves away from our blinkered biochemical levers.

These levers are powerful motivators, due to the imagined results of the action taken and the anticipation of that action's results. But why are they so powerful, and how do they work?

Are you smarter than a rat?

The grand wizard (of Oz, the one with the curtains and the levers) is an amusing metaphor for an area in our brains known as the nucleus accumbens. It is a major part of the brain's pleasure centre, and as such, often pulls our strings (or presses our buttons, or flips our switches, etc.) from behind the scenes.

We think 'we' are the ones in control, making all the decisions, but in reality there is a 'being' behind the curtains controlling (or rather influencing) our decisions without us fully realising it.

The wizard, or the nucleus accumbens, was uncovered through the work done in the late 1950s and early 1960s by two scientists, James Olds and Peter Milner, primarily through experimentation on animals[28].

The way Olds and Milner discovered how the nucleus accumbens works was not the most animal-friendly of methods, but it was effective. Their process involved taking a lab rat and implanting electrodes directly into the animal's brain, specifically its nucleus accumbens, to measure what it specifically did.

The rat would then be given a choice between (A) food and drink, or (B) pressing a button that activated the electrodes that stimulated the nucleus accumbens directly. Now, food and drink are anticipatory rewards that will stimulate the nucleus accumbens in their own right, but the effect of the electrodes stimulating the nucleus accumbens directly was far more pronounced and powerful. What they found was that the rats began to increasingly choose to press the button instead of eating or drinking.

Imagine that – the impact of direct stimulation in this area of the brain was so powerful that rats gave up food and drink just to keep experiencing it. And this is the same pleasure area of the brain that food, sex, our mobile phones and (of course) games impact us.

Olds and Milner deduced that the nucleus accumbens must either be, or be part of, what they came to call the 'pleasure centre' of the brain. And as they observed with the rat's obsession with pressing the button, the centre has a distinct effect on obsession and addiction.

Now you may be thinking at this stage, 'but those are just rats, humans aren't that easily influenced'.

You would be wrong.

A few years later, other researchers repeated Olds and Milner's experiment with humans and found the same thing – worse actually.

Even when the researchers turned off the machine, the participants continued pressing the button. The devices and the participants eventually had to be forcibly removed.

Are you smarter than a dog?

Okay, the rat test was unethical, inserting electrical probes into brains has never ended well in horror movies and we don't recommend trying it at home. So, what about a less invasive approach?

How do we activate the nucleus accumbens without metal probes?

First, close your eyes, as we want you to imagine making your favourite meal. Try and picture it on a plate right in front of you, imagine how it smells and what the first bite will taste like (we personally picture frying a steak, sizzling in butter until it's medium rare…apologies to the vegetarians and vegans out there).

What happened just now in your mouth while you were picturing your favourite meal? Your mouth probably started salivating in anticipation of the imagined meal, right? If not, you probably weren't trying hard enough, or you might not have been conditioned to respond that way to the stimulus we presented.

Being conditioned to a stimulus to get the desired response (like making you salivate when thinking about frying a steak) is Ivan Pavlov's classical conditioning[29]. He first discovered this phenomenon when he was researching the digestive tracts of dogs and noted that the dogs he was researching would drool excessively whenever the lab technician who fed them came into the room – regardless of whether that person had food with them.

This response was the nucleus accumbens activating to a learned response. The dogs had come to associate the lab technician with food, meaning their nucleus accumbens activated whenever they saw him.

Pavlov then went on to test this observation using a metronome (the new stimulus) instead of the lab technician. He would set the metronome ticking only before he fed the dogs (the food was the reward). In the beginning, the dogs would have no response to the metronome (they weren't conditioned to the stimulus yet), but after some time, the dogs began to associate the sound of the metronome with the reward of food.

Soon, Pavlov could introduce the stimulus (the ticking metronome) without the reward (food) and still get the conditioned response (drooling). He believed that this was the fundamental driver behind all motivation and actions, and that, like dogs, we are programmable to respond to learned cause and effect conditions.

This became a major school of thought in psychology with multiple follow-up experiments that tested the same principles – that animals and humans can be 'classically' conditioned to behave in set ways. They showed that we often make these associations between stimuli and rewards naturally ourselves, but that they can also be artificially introduced, by metronome-wielding psychologists, for example.

Are you smarter than yesterday?

Not everyone agreed with Pavlov, though. Another psychologist, B.F. Skinner, believed that classical conditioning was too simplistic to account for the complexities of human behaviour. Simple observation shows that humans do not live their whole lives based on learned stimuli-response loops.

Skinner called his approach operant conditioning[30]. He believed that the best way to understand behaviour is through the lens of cause and effect, and the lessons that we learn from it over time.

The basics of operant conditioning are that we remember the results of our behaviour. If we do something (like touch a hot iron) and receive a negative consequence (we burn our hand), then we are less likely to do it in the future. The opposite being true for positive consequences.

Skinner called this 'reinforcement' and suggested that our behaviour is constantly changing based on our learned experiences of positive and negative reinforcements to our actions. Not only that, but we also respond to a lack of reinforcements, forgetting or changing behaviours if we haven't received reinforcement in some time. This dynamic approach to learning is much more in line with how we actually behave.

In another example of unethical animal experimentation, Skinner studied operant conditioning by placing rats inside what came to be known as the 'Skinner Box', which was essentially a cage that contained a lever that the rat could operate.

As the rats aimlessly moved around Skinner's box, they would occasionally knock the lever, which caused food pellets to appear. Over time, the rats learned that by moving the lever they would get food and they would repeat the action, again and again, to get fed.

Another version of the experiment electrified the box until a rat operated the lever; you can imagine how quickly the rat learned to turn off the electric current once it accidentally nudged the lever the first time.

We can all think of examples of how our own behaviour has been affected by reinforcement over time. As children, we all learn by trial and error, and this practice continues on into adulthood, although by this point we are all mostly just reinforcing already learned lessons rather than actively creating new associations.

For example, if when you were younger, you tried smoking at school, you will have unconsciously weighed up the pros and cons. You may have fallen in with the 'cool' kids and discovered that smoking relaxed you before exams, but you may have also been discovered by your parents or teachers and been punished. Depending on your experiences, you may or may not still be smoking today, as the differing results of your actions will have pushed you in one direction or another.

Every time we do something, we learn something. Many activities will not have a correspondingly apparent positive/negative reinforcement because they are too long-term, but any activity which causes us pleasure or helps us to avoid short-term pain is likely to activate the nucleus accumbens.

We're all obsessive, in some form

If all these factors trigger the nucleus accumbens, what is it doing to react in such a way?

The nucleus accumbens is part of the physiological and psychological reward system that is activated when you anticipate something. This anticipation is usually the expectation to either achieve something good or avoid something bad. In both cases, the feel-good effect is supported by a neurotransmitter chemical, known as dopamine, being released into the nucleus accumbens.

You've probably heard of dopamine; it is the celebrity of neurotransmitters and gets all the press, both positive and negative, for its connection to our sense of pleasure and feelings of anticipation. But it does much more than this, of course, and interacts with other neurotransmitters (like serotonin) to make more complex changes in the brain – but for our purposes, we will simply look at dopamine and its effects on motivation.

Dopamine is the chemical that aids us in learning what feels good – and it's what influences many of our actions.

When this chemical is released from the hypothalamus, it circulates around the brain and serves a great many functions. Dopamine travels through many different paths in the brain, but the main path of interest to us is the mesolimbic dopamine system, of which the nucleus accumbens is a part – making up a large portion of what researchers call the 'pleasure centre' of the human brain.

Advances in technology have improved our understanding of this 'pleasure centre'. Professor Brian Knutson conducted a study exploring blood flow in the brains of people who gambled in a game while inside an fMRI machine[31].

He found that the nucleus accumbens did not activate after the reward had been received (like Olds and Milner hypothesised); it actually activated once the participant started to anticipate a reward or punishment.

And this is very important.

Interestingly, he also found that this activation caused stress in the person, which motivated them to act in a certain way so that they would receive the reward they now dreamed of. This was evident as the nucleus accumbens was activating even when the 'gamblers' lost – the 'near miss' they experienced meant they felt compelled to try over and over again.

Nir Eyal in his book *Hooked: How to Build Habit-Forming Products* has a great phrase describing this psychological effect: 'the stress of desire'[32].

The '*stress of desire*' describes the state we are in when there is a gap between what we anticipate and our current state, and depending on the outcome, the stress we experience because of this gap can either have a positive conclusion or a negative one.

A good example of one of dopamine's effects on us (and the stress of desire) is when we are hungry. We'll repeat the earlier exercise where you picture making your favourite meal and taking that first bite.

If that were real life and you had actually made your favourite meal, you would have anticipated the reward of it tasting good and satiating your hunger. That entire event would be a physical response created with the release of dopamine and endorphins. But as we said, the brain is an amazing organ, and this stimulation can even occur when we imagine or perceive something. Visual stimuli (imagined or real) are enough to activate the nucleus accumbens and the release of dopamine, especially when it has an anticipated reward or outcome we desire.

The nucleus accumbens does have two sides to it though. Our initial examples are of its positive effects, where we feel good when we anticipate a desirable reward. But the other side of the nucleus accumbens is our aversion system.

Loss aversion, demonstrated by Daniel Kahneman and discussed in his bestseller *Thinking, Fast and Slow*, often boils down to the question of choosing the 'lesser of two evils' and that 'if there is even a small chance they may lose what they have earned, people will go to great lengths to protect against the loss'[33].

Kahneman's concept suggests that if an individual is presented with two choices, would they rather gain a discount of €10 or avoid a possible surcharge of €10? In more cases than not, the individual would choose to avoid the surcharge than getting the discount. This is because the anticipation of losing something is sometimes greater than the assured outcome of a discount.

You versus the wizard

Hopefully, you have a good amount of scepticism around all of these models. Human beings are much more complex than the limited number of psychological models we have covered here, but these simple models do help us understand some of the biochemical and psychological factors that influence us every day.

The release of dopamine and the activation of the nucleus accumbens is indeed an invisible wizard in our brains who will often try to affect us to behave in specific ways. This is not a bad thing; it's how we evolved and the most basic way we learn about life and our environment.

But blindly following your instincts and responding only to what might make you feel good is not a good life strategy. The chemical 'pleasure centre' of our brain is focused primarily on short-term benefits and hasn't necessarily evolved alongside us to understand modern goals like not spending your mortgage/rent money on gambling, or not eating every sugared doughnut despite your growing waistline.

Not only that, but the brain will also try to 'trick' you into doing more of an activity by lessening its response to the same stimulus over time (or conversely, making you more accustomed to ever-changing stimuli).

B.F. Skinner in part discovered this with his own version of the Olds and Milner experiment.

Skinner made a food dispenser for pigeons that delivered seeds only sometimes when a button was pushed; this conditioned the pigeon to be more motivated to press the button all the time, just to find out whether it would or wouldn't receive food, in spite of being hungry or not.

As the actions (in this case, the pigeon pressing the button) increase in quantity, these actions run the risk of becoming repetitive. For humans, if the anticipated reward does not vary, or not enough, the outcome can become predictable. Therefore the loop becomes ever increasingly mundane and too repetitive to receive the same levels of stimulation; in other words, it becomes boring.

Additionally, as you may have guessed, this is also where obsessive behaviour can stem from. You need only look at slot machines in a casino to see this type of conditioned behaviour in action. Slot machines are successful, despite their repetitive nature, thanks to the highly variable rewards they can offer that makes us want 'just one more go'.

Dopamine and gamification

So, how does this fit in with marketing gamification?

As you have probably guessed by now, powerful vehicles that influence the release of dopamine are films, videos and games. These mediums are based on visual stimulation and, usually, unexpectedly surprising the viewer. It is the unexpected surprise that activates dopamine release – we gleefully expect the unexpected.

But how can you use these vehicles in marketing? Section 2 will explore this, but we wanted to give a few examples while the concept of dopamine is still fresh in your mind.

For the anticipatory aspect of dopamine, a favourite example of ours in gamifying video marketing is a somewhat older YouTube series,

Will It Blend?[34]. The premise is brilliant, and an amazing illustration of how to gamify the marketing of an incredibly mundane and dull product into something fun and unexpected.

For those unfamiliar with *Will It Blend?* a man in a lab coat throws random objects into the company's latest blender to see if the blender can withstand blending the object. In the case of *Will It Blend?* a 'scientist' would take something like a brand-new iPhone and pose the question of 'will it blend?'. He would then throw in the iPhone and switch on the company's branded blender.

Instantly we are presented and stimulated with a surprise (remember that the stimulation of the nucleus accumbens comes with the anticipation of the outcome, not the actual reward). For new viewers, it is the surprise of watching a man genuinely blend something so valuable and coveted as a smartphone, and the additional surprise that the blender could actually blend the object in question.

The expectation was to find an item that the blender could not blend. The iPhone, in this example, blended just fine into millions and millions of tiny techno-dust particles. The video campaign was a great success with people regularly returning to view what will be blended next.

Gamification and marketing techniques that impact the sense of loss aversion are less obvious though, as most companies do not want these techniques exposed as they can unintentionally appear underhanded and manipulative to customers when they realise they may have been impacted by them. Companies will use them, though, as they are so effective for pushing a sale and will often package them up as helpful messages or customer support to sugarcoat the loss aversion pill.

A good example of this loss aversion technique is the holiday website Booking.com, which regularly uses on-screen messages such as 'There are only 2 hotel rooms left at this price', '15 people are looking at this hotel right now' or 'this hotel was last booked 5 minutes ago'. Companies like this are creating a sense of urgency and action, especially when they combine these messages with free reservation offers to compel their customers to act now or miss out on their dream holiday.

Summary: Chapter 4

The human brain has a 'pleasure centre' which contains the nucleus accumbens; this causes the release of dopamine when we expect to receive a reward or avoid a punishment. Dopamine aids us in learning what feels good, and we are biologically driven to try and repeat that which feels good. Our actions and their associated dopamine releases are learned over time and are reinforced as we keep experiencing them.

However, we also feel 'the stress of desire' when we think that we might not get what we are expecting. This stress increases our likelihood to act in certain ways as we become more knowledgeable about what motivates us and what doesn't.

Next steps:

- Go to your favourite shopping website (or down the high street) and see if you can spot marketing tactics that affect or influence our dopamine release – these may be based on either positive aspects (the expectation of rewards) or negative aspects (the fear of missing out).
- Have you been conditioned to shop in a certain way? Look through your past few months' purchases and see if any patterns show up – why do you keep shopping at these places?

CHAPTER FIVE

The evolution of human needs

Understanding our basic motivators

As we've just seen, our brain's chemical processes can influence us into performing – or not performing – certain actions. This is our brain, the often hidden *'person behind the curtain'* that has guided us from the beginning and has led us to where we are today.

But where has it been leading us? What do we – as humans – really want?

Let's not get carried away at this point and list all the things we want as part of modern society – that will come later. Early humans didn't want alcohol, takeaways, computer games or whatever you're craving right now. The needs of the earliest humans were a lot more animalistic, and while our basic needs haven't changed much, modern society and technology have certainly shifted our motivational priorities.

Let's start at the very beginning, with a fictional early-man, who will help us show how humanity started out.

So, what does this 'early-man' want?

Physiological needs

Early-man needs to stay hydrated and (hopefully) eat nutritious foods; he also needs air to breathe, needs to maintain optimum body temperature and needs a certain amount of sleep to keep functioning optimally. This is basic biology for all humans to survive, to stay at peak condition to continue hunting/gathering and to live as long as possible.

Thankfully, modern man doesn't need to hunt, but we still require energy and nutrition for survival, and without these basic requirements any human would die. Avoiding death is the ultimate motivator, and the human brain has many methods to prod you into taking action if you start to ignore these basic physiological survival needs.

Safety and shelter

Early-man also needs a safe place to sleep that offers protection from the elements and other hunters. When we were hunter-gatherers, we might have spent a long time trying to find suitable shelter and protect it. This is important as, without it, we would die of exposure to the elements and predators.

Modern man has similar needs; we still seek shelter, like our homes, and feel safe within them, working to keep them functional and taking every measure possible to protect them from intruders. Even outside of our shelter, we will all (to varying degrees) avoid dangerous situations and take steps to maintain an optimum temperature with heating and appropriate clothing.

Intimacy

Finally, humans desire intimacy; on a primal level it ensures that we reproduce. As humans, on a macro scale, we actively seek out suitable partners for the purpose of reproduction. With this activity also comes the need to care for the offspring produced and to ensure a higher chance of survival for that offspring. This is our basic need for interaction and empathy between each other and leads to more complex actions that require teamwork, influencing and compromise to achieve certain desired outcomes.

We are still animals at heart

These three animalistic needs are what make up our core evolutionary levers and still have an impact on modern-day motivation. Frederick Herzberg[35] developed the two-factor theory of motivation that looks at how our original motivational instincts still play a factor in the modern-day work environment.

Herzberg observed and interviewed over 200 engineers to understand what made them happy or unhappy in their work. From these interviews he split their motivations into two groups:

1) *'Motivation Factors'* are the positive psychological factors that provide increased motivation, such as recognition and/or competence in a task.
2) *'Hygiene Factors'* are those that if they are not fulfilled, lead to decreased motivation and workplace dissatisfaction.

These *'Hygiene Factors'* are directly linked to our evolutionary motivators like hunger, physical safety, temperature and (job) security – and their absence acts as a blocker to any positive motivational factors that may be present. For example, you cannot enjoy a creative challenge if you are freezing, can't afford food or are in an unsafe environment.

This is important to remember, because while our physiological needs will drive us to perform certain actions, their absence will also stop enjoyment of other activities and the desire to perform them – this is directly relevant for workplace gamification where you are trying to motivate employees, but it is still quite relevant (although somewhat less controllable) for marketing gamification. You won't get your customers to engage with your campaigns while they're freezing to death or worried they're about to lose their job.

Humanity, however, isn't just a singular person or family. We are not just lone animals wandering the plains looking for our next meal or a safe space. We crave a partner, children, friends, a tribe, a community.

And this is where human needs and our motivations to fulfil them takes a leap forward.

Greater than their sum: Community motivators

Communities have a number of advantages, mostly around safety; such as the safety of larger numbers, the ability to divide up labour or increase the collection of resources, and the support of others with injuries or sickness. Due to these benefits, communities help us to maintain a baseline of Herzberg's hygiene factors.

This is why community is one of the main reasons why humanity has had the breathing room to start chasing other more complex needs in the first place.

Communities are good for us, but as individuals, we can't just take from the community, we must also contribute to it. Each person (especially in the early tribal days of mankind) needs to provide a level of value that is somewhat equal to that which they extract from the wider group if they are to remain in that community.

As a very basic example, if you work as a gatherer for the tribe you've joined, you are expected to spend most of your day in the woods collecting food, which you will share with the tribe. In exchange, you will get to eat meat from the hunters, sleep around the fire and feel safe in the knowledge that if you are ill, others will take care of you until you are better.

This sounds great, but if you don't keep up your end of the (community) bargain, you run the risk of being rejected from the group and having to fend for yourself alone – something you may be unable to do after having lived within a community.

In modern times this is as relevant as ever. Each of us has to work in exchange for payment, which can be exchanged again for the fruits of other people's labour. You might get away with not doing much work for a while, but when you're eventually caught out, you'll probably lose your job and struggle to find a new one without a good reference. If you lose your job, you may have a safety net (savings, family, government relief), but when this fails, what then? Could you survive without a community around you? How long do you think you could feed yourself or stay warm without one?

These communities start with our personal family and friendship groups, up to the more formal workplace communities and even to our status as citizens of our chosen countries or residents in foreign countries. Each community will have its own requirements, its own benefits and its own consequences if those requirements aren't met.

You can easily see how a community and each individual's maintenance of their place inside a community has quickly become one of our greatest motivators, especially when targeted with gamification; in particular when individuals seek to join a successful community or take part in activities that successful communities are doing.

Give and take: Socio-economic motivators

The give-and-take barter system that accompanies our communities is what made up early trade, a loose organisation of understandings and individual roles that made society function and progress.

But as humanity developed, so did our communities and the complexities of our relationships. We invented currency, hierarchies and laws to position and govern individuals within the wider community. These developments have made the world what it is today and bring with it several new motivational factors to consider.

So, what do we want in this more complex world?

We still value food, warmth and safety. We are still influenced by our own biochemistry to chase short-term gratification. But as society has changed, so has the way we need to fulfil our basic needs. For example, we no longer need to hunt for food, so we now need to earn money to acquire food.

This fundamental change in how we meet our basic needs means that we have moved into an economic model of motivation. Everything has a price nowadays whether it's our time, attention or ability – and some of us have learned the best ways to maximise our gains while minimising our losses.

The majority of modern motivational theory is focused on these economic models of motivation, believing that most humans based their unconscious and conscious decision-making on how to maximise their assets.

Two theories stand out when discussing socio-economic motivation that will help us to understand better some of the more complicated (and often automated) calculations that occur in our heads.

Expectancy theory

One of the key socio-economic motivational models was put forward by Victor H. Vroom: *Expectancy Theory*[36].

Vroom believed that we are motivated to do an action based on our expectation of a reward or punishment. This is similar to the conditioning theories we discussed in the previous chapter, but Vroom went one step further, suggesting that the amount of motivation would be altered based on our:

- **Expectancy**: Belief that a reward or punishment is likely if we act in a certain way, specifically the probability of it happening. For example, 'if I turn up to work today, I am pretty sure that I will be paid'.
- **Instrumentality**: Belief that if an action is performed well, the likelihood of a reward or the amount of reward will increase (and the reverse for punishment). For example, 'if I do a really good job serving this table their dinner, I believe I will get a larger tip'.
- **Valence**: Valuation of the reward or punishment. For example, if the reward for attending an hour-long seminar is a €10 gift voucher, an individual would weigh up how much they value the €10 gift voucher against the time cost of attending a one-hour seminar.

This is a much more mature thought model than classical or operant conditioning and reflects the complex nature of rewards and their associated values in modern society.

Vroom made it clear that these calculations were constantly being made by each individual (both unconsciously and consciously) and that they were based on each individual's perceptions of value.

This individual perception of value is what makes us unique and is the reason why some people will happily spend an hour cleaning their beloved car while others will pay for a machine to do it for them quickly.

What is interesting, though, is how each individual arrives at their value calculation. Each component of Vroom's calculation is highly subjective to the individual and will be influenced based on their upbringing, demographics, life experiences, even their mood at the time.

Expectancy theory is what the majority of modern society is based upon, as we all make constant mental calculations in our head for each action or inaction that we take. Such as whether we go to work today, whether we buy that latest gadget, whether we eat that three-day-old leftover or whether we listen to our friend tell the same story to us for the eighth time.

Every customer will have a different perception of value and will react differently to your offerings. If you misinterpret what customers value, or you don't make the offer clear enough to them so they understand its value, then they will not be interested. It is for this reason that we have outlined certain steps in Section 3 to help you properly map out and test your assumptions.

The endowment effect

The second key socio-economic motivational model is the *endowment effect*. This is the theory that not only do we overvalue the things that we already own, but that we also disproportionately fear to lose what we already own too. The endowment effect can have a significant impact on expectancy theory, as it massively skews each individual's value calculations.

We overvalue what we have

As an example, a study done by Richard Thaler et al.[37] found that once participants were given an object (in this case a mug) and ownership had been established, the compensation they required in order to sell the object tended to be twice as high as the amount they were willing to pay to acquire/buy the object.

This was because the participants had overvalued the (expected) value, based on what they went through to get the object in the first place, and the fact that the object was now in their possession. This is compared to the other participants who had missed out on the acquisition and had not skewed their value judgements. This is interesting, as you would expect that those without a mug would want one of their own, but this is not the case.

This is a simple example, but the same rule holds true in our daily lives. When we own something, we become strangely attached to it, unwilling to part with it unless we are given something much more valuable than the object we own. Can you imagine how this may impact expectancy theory? Or any of the other motivational factors that we've discussed so far?

This phenomenon is universal, but you often see the evidence with large purchases like cars and houses. This can also be linked to another phenomenon called the 'sunk cost effect', which is when an individual who has invested time/money into something becomes increasingly attached to it beyond the point of reason.

Gamification often uses this to good effect. Players will build up a collection of badges, points, achievements or progress in a particular system, and will then be loath to leave them behind.

Loyalty cards that businesses give you (either the digital points cards from big retailers or the physical stamps to get a free coffee or haircut) are a good example of this. These may seem like throwaway gimmicks, but there is a reason they are so popular. Once you have a loyalty card in your pocket, you are much more likely to keep shopping with the provider to keep building your points.

We fear losing what we have

When we overvalue what we own, we also disproportionately fear losing what we own. People will go out of their way to ensure that they don't lose access to what they perceive as their property.

This is valuable information for marketing gamification in the services industry, as you can use this as a tool to keep customers using your services over time. Be warned, though, that like most gamification principles, if the player feels like you are doing this for selfish reasons, then they will punish you by leaving.

A fun example of this is 'The Most Dangerous Writing App', a web tool that deletes your writing if you take too long a break. Users sign up and set a time limit for their writing session; if they stop writing for more than the allotted time, the words start disappearing from the page. Other examples of this are common in fitness and language learning apps where your fitness or fluency points degrade over time if you don't keep up practising or logging your exercises.

These examples are successful because the users of these tools can see the benefit to them and their goals; writers want to write and not lose their words, while language learners and fitness fanatics want to progress and not slide backwards in their achievements.

If you contrast this to a loyalty scheme that takes away your points if you don't use them over time, you are able to see which is effective and which isn't. If you own a loyalty card with 1,000 points, but for every day you don't add a point you lose a point, you will be annoyed rather than compelled to buy more. Why? Because your goal may be to save rather than spend.

The missing piece

These last two chapters have looked at the biological, chemical, evolutionary and even sociological reasons why we feel compelled to act in certain ways. Our brain chemistry rewards us when we seek pleasure or avoid pain; our animalistic nature seeks to protect itself from danger and find shelter and food; our modern society motivates us to conform to societal standards and maintain or improve our position in that society.

All this makes a certain amount of sense, but it feels like something is missing, right?

The theories we've covered treat us like unthinking automatons, endlessly calculating values to work out the best possible route to pleasure. But how do we work out these values? We've already said they are highly subjective, so what are they based on?

What we've discussed so far assumes that humans make their decisions based on past information, but this gives little insight into *why* people do what they do in the first place, besides an (animalistic) short-term gain/loss maximisation/minimisation drive.

All the calculations we do are supposedly based on an individual's perceptions of value. But where do these perceptions come from? What makes an individual value one thing more than another?

For gamification, we are much more interested in these questions. Understanding our basic needs and brain chemistry is important but isn't really something that we as marketers will be influencing much with our campaigns. We need to think at a higher level.

What we need to know next is how these basic needs have developed in modern humans, and how we as individuals rank and assess their value. Once we understand this, we can start to use these value judgements to build the motivational levers of your gamification strategy.

Summary: Chapter 5

Humans are driven by basic motivators like safety, shelter and survival. These basic motivators will always be important to us, and without them, we will not pursue more advanced needs.

Our advanced needs have grown in complexity as humans have built communities and systems of trade. These communities allow us to share resources but also mean we have a whole new tier of needs that motivate us to maintain our position within society (working, socialising, remaining within the law, etc.).

But, as our needs and motivations keep developing, so do the complexity of the calculations and assumptions we must make when weighing up choices in everyday life.

Despite our assumptions, the reality is that everyone values things differently and it is these differences and their implications that we will cover in the next chapter.

Next steps:

- How many loyalty schemes are you a part of? Think about why you joined and why you are still a member. Do they influence you to do more business with that organisation? If you don't use the scheme anymore, why are you still a member and why do you keep the loyalty card? Do you feel tension when you think about just throwing those points away?

- Consider what you own, how much you spent on acquiring it and what its current value is to you, either monetary or emotionally. What would it take for you to part with it and what feelings occur in you when you consider this?

CHAPTER SIX

Motivation in a developed world

The basic drives that we've covered so far are best summed up as how we as humans manage to keep afloat and survive. Living in such a way can be a static existence that is only really given meaning through material acquisition. Think of the old anecdotal stereotype of the sad, rich man with no friends or dreams, just money for its own sake.

This can work for people in the short term, as they find pleasure in extrinsic rewards like salaries, owning the latest device, having the newest gaming console and so on, but we soon begin to feel empty as human beings if this is all we strive for.

What we really want and need are *intrinsic* rewards.

These are rewards where you internally feel good about an accomplishment, as opposed to the extrinsic, temporary, rewards of owning 'stuff'. What intrinsic rewards we need and how highly we value them can be different for everyone, but it is the fundamental WHY of every individual's drive in their life, and it's what marketing gamification focuses on leveraging.

What we need to understand then are these universal 'whys' of humanity.

But first, we need to consider an initial framework on which we can hang these 'whys'; those that go beyond the basics of survival; a model that we can use going forwards and something that considers not just the animalistic needs we all feel, but also one that identifies and incorporates our higher order needs in the modern world.

This is where Abraham Maslow comes in[38].

Motivation and Maslow's hierarchy of needs

If you're in marketing, you're probably already familiar with Maslow's pyramid, but we encourage you to refresh your memory because this is what a lot of this book's structure will be based on going forward.

Maslow came up with a model that fits all human needs into a pyramid. This structure was designed to show all the needs in a hierarchy, with our most basic needs at the bottom, and each tier is then supporting a more complex need above it.

What this means is that each tier or floor in the pyramid is a prerequisite for the next floor. So without adequately achieving the first floor, you cannot comfortably move to the second floor.

This is not to say that each floor is gated and that if you haven't achieved safety, you cannot achieve belonging. But rather that if safety isn't sufficiently achieved, then the process of belonging will be significantly harder and more draining to keep up, both physically and emotionally. And all subsequent floors will become exponentially draining if the bottom ones aren't appropriately fulfilled first. Think of it as an actual building; you could build a second floor on top of a shaky first floor, but you'd never sleep comfortably in it.

Maslow's hierarchy fits perfectly then as it follows the same journey of needs as those that have already been covered so far. We can see how each stage occurred in human civilisation, but also how each is important to us in our daily lives. We cannot achieve our potential without climbing this pyramid, both as individuals and as a species.

Note that it is important to understand Maslow's hierarchy fully for your progress in this book as we will in part be using the various building blocks of Maslow's pyramid to describe the different ways you can gamify your marketing. In our case, we will build a gamification tower and show you how to use the building blocks based on Maslow's pyramid to create this framework.

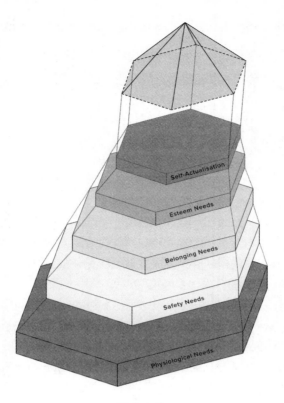

Figure 1.

Each building block will have its own game mechanics that you can use in your marketing, and Section 3 will teach you how to glue these blocks together to make an effective gamification solution.

First, though, we will go through each tier of Maslow's pyramid and explain its purpose and how it motivates us to act in certain ways.

Floor 1: Physiological needs

Our physiological needs form the basis for a person and are paramount to our survival. If these needs are not met, then our body will ultimately fail and die. These are very straightforward, and we all understand them at a primal level.

Physiological needs can be split into three categories: Metabolic, Elemental and Sexual.

- **Metabolic** needs are the basic requirements our bodies have for survival: air – breathing, water – thirst, and food – hunger. Without these three our bodies will die.
- **Elemental** needs are our requirements for warmth and shelter, such as clothing, access to heat and a place to store both.
- **Sexual** needs are the base instincts to procreate to guarantee the survival of the species, but also the base aspect that drives us to seek each other out for comfort.

You're probably wondering now, what do these have to do with gamifying marketing?

Well on face value, not a whole lot to be honest. Ethically speaking, it would be a very bad idea to gamify any of these needs in real life. The importance, though, of knowing and understanding these basic needs is that if they are not fulfilled for an individual, then no experience you come up with will work.

You should also be aware that there are abstractions that we can take away from these base physiological needs that you can build to simulate other physiological needs.

Games and gamified experiences do this by building in artificial physiological needs like health bars, lose conditions and scarcity of resources to represent and evoke the same drives in us. We know that we want to survive and not lose/die, and instinctively understand game concepts that revolve around these ideas.

Floor 2: Safety

If a person is warm and fed, then their next concern and step up Maslow's pyramid will be their safety and security. Safety, like physiology, is divided into subgroups: Physical safety and Economic safety.

- **Physical safety** is anything to do with health, wellbeing, personal security against disaster, violence, war, famine, pestilence, etc.
- **Economic safety** moves us into the modern world, where people want job security, insurance, savings accounts, mortgages, taxes etc.

These first two floors of physical needs and safety are the animalistic needs that we touched on previously and are (hopefully) fulfilled in most of the customers that you'll be targeting with your gamification marketing.

Like physiological needs, you should not be gamifying safety needs directly as that would be immoral (and probably illegal), but you can instead gamify elements of your marketing to mimic these needs for the player. Both physiological and safety needs are highly motivating when targeted but are also a bit of a moral grey area as it is easy to create obsessive systems like gambling when you target them directly.

Chapter 12 will further explore what game elements and designs you can incorporate to evoke these pseudo-physiological needs in players, and how they will be motivated to fill this gap by going through your experience.

Floor 3: Belonging

Belonging to a group or a community is a very strong motivator and covers our needs for connection with family, friends, colleagues or romantic partners. Being part of a group offers security, safety in numbers and can help us fulfil our basic needs through the group's asset sharing.

Importantly, though, this floor is not just about extrinsic, physical needs like food, sex and safety that a group can provide. This floor starts the transition from extrinsic (external) needs to intrinsic (internal) needs.

These intrinsic needs stem from having an intimate connection with those around you and gaining a sense of personal meaning through your identity in the groups you belong to and your position within these groups.

This is a strong motivator, and the lack of it is equally strong. Many people go out of their way to join desirable groups or avoid losing their membership in groups. All of this is to gain status, access to other people or to avoid or lessen the prospect of loneliness or exclusion.

Think of the joy you feel being the 'funny one' in your group of friends, or the 'tech expert' at work. Do you take pride in being a good mother, or a loving son? Are you hurt when you don't get invited to a friend's wedding, or when you have an argument with someone and they stop talking to you?

All of these feelings demonstrate the power of belonging, and you would be surprised at what you would do to protect or grow your standing in the groups you belong to. This is because a lot of who we are and how we see ourselves is tied to our identity in these groups, and we will often act in ways to stay consistent with our self-identity.

From a gamification perspective, belonging is the most common need we find when we see clubs, exclusive groups, loyalty programmes and so on. People inherently wish to be part of something that they have been excluded from which they can see value in or that they think they would fit into.

Chapter 11 will explore how you can use belonging to motivate players, and which game elements most appeal to people who respond to this need.

Floor 4: Esteem

Every person has an intrinsic need to be respected. This is both respect from outside by a community or group that they are part of, but also internally in the form of self-respect and self-esteem.

Both of these are linked, as external esteem is given or earned from a group which evokes a sense of self-esteem in an individual. This links to the belonging floor as many people build their esteem through their identity within a group, e.g. being a good family member, friend, mentor, employee, etc. A person will tie their esteem to how their status rises and falls in a group, motivating them to behave in certain ways.

But it's not all about how other people see us; a person's sense of self-respect for who they are and what they do will also build esteem. This is how we judge ourselves for doing a good job or for acting in a way that is consistent with our self-identity. This is different for each person, but can largely be bucketed under 'being successful at a task that we care about'.

In gamification terms, this is where concepts such as acknowledging accomplishments comes from, and giving rewards through status. These are in turn associated with mastery and competence in a task or skill. Chapter 10 will explore how effective this lever can be when gamifying anything that has inherent challenges and progression.

Floor 5: Self-Actualisation

Self-actualisation is the uppermost floor of Maslow's pyramid and can be seen as the endgame area when it comes to an individual's needs. This floor is when an individual has satisfied all their lower needs enough that they can focus fully on reaching their own potential. Maslow believes that this is the goal we all strive for.

It's important to remember that while society at large may currently guide us to think that self-actualisation is akin to being wealthy, powerful and famous, in reality, it is a choice that you as an individual may want (and need) to feel fulfilled. For others, it may be becoming a loving parent, or an Olympic athlete or very simply an accomplished gardener.

As Maslow describes it: '*What a man can be, he must be*'[39].

Self-actualisation is the holy grail of motivation once cracked and is what many of the most effective gamification solutions target effectively. But you may be scratching your head at this point, because unlike the other floors of Maslow's pyramid, self-actualisation is a bit 'fluffy'.

Have you ever heard someone describe themselves as 'self-actualised'? We instinctively understand the need to be alive, to be safe, to belong, to feel important. But what does self-actualisation really mean? We're going to need to break it down further before we can start effectively targeting it with gamification methods.

Making self-actualisation less 'fluffy'

A good place to start when looking to expand on Maslow's work is with other models in positivist psychology, specifically with Daniel Pink's *Drive*[40] (based in part on Edward Deci and Richard M. Ryan's *Self-Determination Theory*[41]).

Pink reviewed the existing motivational psychology literature and combined it with his own observations in business. He concluded that existing models were too transactional and did not reflect the true nature of human interactions and were therefore unsuitable for the modern world.

He argued that the traditional approaches of motivational psychology were only effective at motivating us in the most basic tasks, but were useless when it came to more complex or creative tasks.

Because of this, he went on to expand Maslow's hierarchy, seeing that it had the potential to explain the complexities behind why we do things, but, like us, concluded that self-actualisation was too 'fluffy' a term.

So Pink created a variation of self-actualisation with three additional 'floors': *Purpose, Mastery* and *Autonomy*.

These three aspects try to explain why we do what we do, beyond our more primal needs. If we have purpose in our lives, we are motivated to continue down that path. If we strive to master a skill or a task that is worthwhile, we are motivated to continue and improve. If we are autonomous and are able to choose our own path, we are motivated to explore and are empowered by our decision-making power to keep going.

Let's examine each substage in more detail:

- **Floor 5-A: Purpose**

  Pink describes purpose as our desire to do things in service of something larger than ourselves. He argues that we all intrinsically want to do things that matter and that 'make a difference'. This has a big impact on workplace motivation (Pink's main target for his book), but also on marketing too. Why do people buy your products/services? What bigger picture are they serving? This may be impossible for some businesses, but purpose is one of the key motivational levers that if targeted correctly will attract dedicated and engaged customers to your business. Chapter 7 will look more at what purpose is in marketing gamification.

- **Floor 5-B: Mastery**

  Mastery is the need to improve at the things that matter to us. Pink argues that we love to get better at things and that we enjoy the satisfaction from personal achievement and progress (you can see how this links to esteem). The problem is finding the level of difficulty that is appropriate for each individual; too easy and you won't improve, too hard and you won't be able to progress. Many marketers fail at targeting mastery effectively because they either get the difficulty wrong, or they try to build mastery in an area that customers don't care about. Chapter 8 will explore mastery in gamification further and show you how to target it effectively.

- **Floor 5-C: Autonomy**

  Lastly, autonomy is the need to direct your own life and work. To be fully motivated, you must be able to control what you do, when you do it, and who you do it with. Pink gives examples of this in the workplace, citing Google's working practices that allow its engineers to use work time to pursue private projects that have made a great impact on the company. But autonomy can also have an impact on marketing. Customers like to feel in control, but by forcing your customers down specific pathways (especially ones with dead ends), you are likely frustrating them and forcing them to go elsewhere. Be warned, though, that too much autonomy can be just as dangerous; Chapter 9 will explore this fully.

These three drives – linked to our basic survival needs and our instincts to seek out like-minded communities and achieve recognition – are what sustains us and drives us forward in life.

Importantly for this book, these are the factors we need to consider when creating gamification experiences. The point of understanding these abstract intrinsic needs, long-term and short-term, is that when you are gamifying an experience, you will need to understand what the personal objectives are of your target audience.

By understanding who your audience is, you can then start to understand what their core levers are – what needs they respond best to. Once you know this, you can then create gamified experiences that appeal to these needs and influence your customers to behave in certain ways – ways that will benefit both of you.

Connecting drives, habits and rewards

We now know and understand the core levers of our audience, and how these are framed within Maslow's hierarchy, Deci and Ryan's self-determination theory and Pink's Drive expansion upon that. So, we can connect this with how our neurobiology, and how marketing, thereupon builds habit-forming loops that we invest in and engage us with (intrinsic) rewards.

One such model to help us connect these is the 'Hooked Model'[42] (Figure 2), created by Nir Eyal. It is especially useful when using both it and Maslow's pyramid as lenses to look at how rewards work, because the model gives us a clearer understanding of where motivation arises on a biochemical level. The model may also be recognisable to those of you who know a similar one in the customer-marketing world; the Customer Decision Journey (CDJ). Yet again this is a looped journey that forms a habit within an individual.

The Hooked Model explores the loop that is created to form a habit. It starts with a Trigger; either an extrinsic or intrinsic trigger, something the individual requires externally or something the individual desires internally. The trigger causes the desired Action to be taken by the individual, which in turn leads to a Reward. To bring it back to neuroscience, and Eyal's own term, *the stress of desire* – the stimulation and anticipation that causes dopamine to occur in this section of the Hooked Model – this is the trigger that causes the action and the anticipation of the reward. Once the action has occurred the individual is Rewarded, the reward is purely representational of the action

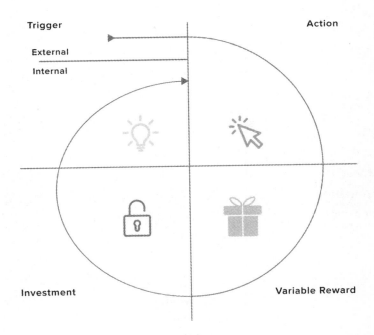

Figure 2.

they've taken. The reward, therefore, links to the 'final' step, which is Investment. This is what the individual has invested, either emotionally, financially, temporally or intellectually. We say 'final', as it is a cycle, and the next step is back to a Trigger that stems out of the previous Investment step.

For those unacquainted with the customer decision journey (Figure 3), it reads just like the Hooked Model. The customer starts with a trigger; generally a perceived need for something, a desire is stimulated. They evaluate their need, which now becomes a perceived level of wanting, the stress of desire as it were. The action takes place at the moment of purchase for the customer. Next, the experience of the purchased item, the perceived expectations of the experience – are they positive or negative in reference to the anticipation that the customer felt? This experience is what then informs the next decision journey, the investment that the customer placed on the acquired item.

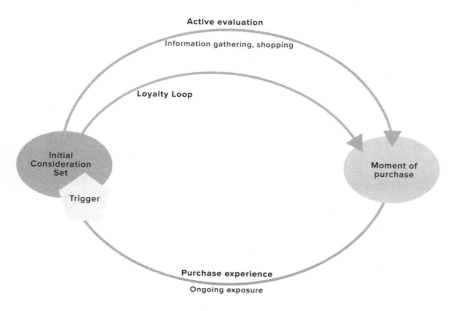

Figure 3.

A great example that ties all of this together is the idea of the mystery collectable. These come in different forms, such as a Loot Crate, or a Loot Box, or a card pack or even the scratch packs for lotteries. Individuals who engage in these are given the full voluntary choice of going for it or not. They generally do, as the monetary investment is low, the ability to do so is very easy, the surprise is worthwhile and the reward is likely something they will enjoy. This is due to either the climax the experience offers, or the renewed interest and continued investment it offers. Regardless of which, they will likely return again to try their 'luck' the next time round. This is also how addictive or obsessive behaviour is created, so be careful. Think of slot machines in casinos.

It's important to note at this point that so far we've looked mostly at the positive aspects of human needs/motivation. But you should know that in the short term these motivators can be flipped, creating very acute needs that align more with avoiding a loss of confidence, security, safety, inclusiveness and others mentioned in the first four floors of Maslow's hierarchy.

You may be thinking this sounds negative, and we've even used the word negative in our descriptions when explaining the various floors. And you'd be right, but this is where we drive the point home in making sure you understand the differences between long-term benefits and short-term hardships.

In gamification, a short period of difficulty can be a strong motivator. It can often be used as that initial push to get the player involved in the experience. They can wish to avoid not being part of an exclusive group, and instead join for the long-term benefits. They may even feel the push to try their luck and chance rolling the dice to create a meaningful long-term connection with someone.

All of these elements need to have a short-term stressful piece and long-term benefit. If you as the creator choose to push the 'negative' elements too far to achieve a certain outcome, then you run the risk of flipping the element to a long-term disadvantage, which leads to demotivation and loss of engagement.

Linking to marketing-gamification

In marketing, one of our main underlying goals is to get customers to want what our organisations are offering. Depending on the stage of the marketing/sales funnel (or journey, or whatever marketing term you're using), this could be through raising brand awareness, redesigning products or tinkering with messaging so that you are more appealing to specific audiences.

But where most marketers go wrong is that they don't really understand what their customers want. This often means that they offer their customers the wrong thing, or more often, they offer the right thing in the wrong way.

This is why we've used the last three chapters to give you a quick and dirty overview of motivational psychology, covering the basic elements of what we want as humans and why we want them.

Many people will already get this, especially if you have a background in marketing, but very few can clearly articulate it and action it in their marketing strategies. What this book will give you is the tools to action these customer needs. Take some of the examples we have come across in our own experience:

- 'We sell luxury cars', no, you sell status – which links to belonging and esteem.
- 'We provide access to our gym equipment', no, you sell fitness – which links to mastery and esteem.
- 'We sell green energy', no, you sell sustainability – which links to purpose and belonging.

Each of these examples has an obvious 'product', but what you need to do is look at what need that product is serving. Which floor of Maslow/

Pink's model-pyramid are you hitting when you solve the customer's problem?

Section 2 will help you to identify these needs across your different customers – linking the various floors of Maslow/Pink's model-pyramid to customer needs – and how to use the tools we'll cover in Section 3 to target these needs effectively.

Our methodology is about engaging with your customers in a meaningful way. This means identifying relevant needs and better aligning your products/services with those needs through gamification techniques.

Do this right, and you'll have a loyal following of engaged customers who know and feel like you understand them. They will do business with you because it is in their best interest and suits their needs. Do this wrong, and that following will (rightfully) try to burn your 'house' down for trying to manipulate them. They will see through your attempts to artificially encourage them to act in certain ways and will punish you for it.

The tools we'll cover have been used successfully by organisations worldwide to better engage their customers, and we'll show you how to do the same yourself.

Summary: Chapter 6

Maslow's pyramid successfully incorporates the basic animalistic needs we all have in the first two levels (physical needs and safety) and the community needs in the third level (belonging). Maslow's pyramid then adds on two additional levels for esteem and self-actualisation, which can be further broken down by Pink's model into purpose, mastery and autonomy.

These 'floors' of the pyramid explain our various needs and motivations. As marketers, you should be trying to identify these needs in your customers and orient your business and its products/services to fulfil these needs.

In the coming section, we will divide the various gamification tools and methods by these motivational floors so you can properly target them to your customers.

Next steps:

- List your organisation's main purpose – what does it do for its customers? Now go through the floors of Maslow's pyramid and identify which floors your organisation fulfils (it can be multiple).
- Now do the same for your main competitors; are they targeting other floors with their marketing or product features? Does their messaging promise to fulfil certain needs that yours doesn't? Many companies we examine in this way realise their competitors are better at appealing to their customer's needs for purpose and belonging.

SECTION TWO

Tools

After Section 1, you should now know what gamification and games are, and the basics of motivational psychology that we will be using in this book. Most importantly, you should know about Maslow's hierarchy of needs, and Pink's Drive theory that enhances it.

What we will show you in Section 2 is that gamification is a method and a toolset that can allow you to sync your marketing with these fundamental human drives – all while ensuring that it is both challenging and enjoyable for the player. This is because we connect better and more efficiently with things we enjoy, that engage us, that hook us into a worthwhile experience.

Each chapter in this section will explore a different floor of Maslow's pyramid, showing you how it relates to gamification marketing and the game mechanics you can use to leverage it.

You'll need this knowledge for the final section, as each tactic that we show you is a building block you can use to create what we call *The Tower of Gamification* framework (we will be showing you how to build your gamification tower in Section 3).

Why a tower?

Basically, it's a useful visual metaphor for what we're trying to achieve. It works across a great many disciplines and interests. A tower instantly evokes an image; you are probably able to imagine one right now, such as the Leaning Tower of Pisa. It can also be a playful image of a LEGO tower, which applies to people of any age.

It also has a strong connection with games, for example for anyone who's played any role-playing, dungeon game like *Diablo* or *Castlevania*.

Regardless of the connection, each person will instantly know why a tower is a brilliant allegory for a gamified journey.

Let's imagine this tower, then.

You're building the tower for your players to ascend. This tower has different floors as your players progress. Each floor may have different challenges and rewards depending on how you want to engage your players. Your job is to design and build this tower, populating it with the raw materials, the building blocks that are the gamification elements that you will need to really attract customers and players.

One thing to keep in the back of your mind while you're working your way through this section is that you don't have to include every element and every mechanic all the time. Different problems require different solutions at various stages in the tower as your player's motivations and needs will change as they progress on their journey.

So, what better place to start your tower with than with the stairs that lead up to its heights? We call these the 'Staircase of Purpose'. Because how else will people progress?

CHAPTER SEVEN

Building your tower –
The staircase of Purpose

What is purpose in gamification? How does it motivate?

Purpose is something that we all crave in our lives.

Purpose is what energises people to move forward. It's the reason people return to an activity day after day, tirelessly working on it, even without any external incentives. This is because purpose is an intrinsic motivator, and possibly one of the most powerful ones we will explore.

Think about the difference between a customer who truly believes in your products compared to one who just sees them as another commodity. Who would you prefer?

This is because purpose offers meaning to an individual's life, and the grander and more relevant that feeling is, the more connected they will feel to it. It is the desire to contribute to something outside of ourselves, to create a lasting effect on those around us, to be part of something greater than we would be if we stayed solitary. Our actions don't have to directly impact our purpose to be effective either; they just need to be aligned.

This is different for everyone, from doing a good job for your boss, to donating to charity or to raising a child, and so on. Not only that, but a person will simultaneously have multiple 'purposes' that will change over time too.

This is the reason we've placed purpose as one of the first motivational levers of our gamification tower model, as it is a core desire and need for everyone. If you can get purpose right, your players will forgive a lot of flaws.

But beware, purpose is one of the more difficult aspects of gamification to get right!

You may be thinking this is because purpose is impossible to manufacture, right? You can't convince someone to take up a 'purpose' that helps your business, can you? Correct, but what you can do is align your goals with your player's purpose.

Wikipedia needs little introduction and shows us how lots of individuals can come together, drawn by a common need and desire for purpose. Wikipedia ticks a great many of the boxes we've just highlighted that are required when developing purpose in an activity or campaign.

However, Wikipedia is an odd example if you think about it; nobody would ever have thought the concept would work. Consider it for a moment, an open-source, free, online encyclopaedia, that has thousands of people all over the world working on it daily, and no one gets paid to do it. In fact, it actually requests donations from the people who value it the most. Had you proposed this type of a system to someone 20 years ago (the late 20th Century), they would probably have called you crazy.

What Wikipedia shows us is that people desire to do something that brings meaning to themselves and others. To be in the service of a cause that is greater than themselves and of their own choosing. Moreover, this is true in all aspects of life, especially when it comes to your gamification marketing campaigns.

As Daniel Pink mentions in his book *Drive*:

'[The science shows that] the secret to high performance isn't our biological drive or our reward-and-punishment drive, but our third drive – our deep-seated desire to direct our own lives, to extend and expand our abilities, and to live a life of purpose.'[43]

Purpose offers us intrinsic value; this value is seen as there being meaning behind an action, and the action should in itself create value for the individual and others around them. This is what elevates it to a higher status, of serving a higher purpose beyond yourself.

This is why we chose to use the analogy of the staircase in our tower framework to illustrate purpose.

One step at a time

What do staircases and purpose have to do with one another, though?

We know that when your players find purpose, it elevates them, and that's why we use the image of a staircase. This is also the reason why purpose is our first motivational lever when building a gamified campaign using our tower framework.

Imagine your players are going through the gamified experience that you've created for them. Each stage in the tower is a different level for them to work through that challenges them and lets them discover new elements and aspects of your brand and their connection to it.

But how are they moving between each level, what is driving them from the ground to the apex of your tower? Purpose is the frame that allows players to ascend along the various stages of your campaign, and thus we have a staircase.

Without a strong frame, a solid meaning behind the actions that they are taking, there is no reason for them to continue. As with the example of Wikipedia, each person involved with it knows and feels that there is a compelling meaning behind their commitment to the platform. Without any promise of an extrinsic reward, thousands of people go through a multitude of entries on Wikipedia every day regardless. They do this because they believe that every step they take as individuals adds to the collective value of Wikipedia. Their sense of purpose grows with each action they take; and to sustain the metaphor a bit, with every step on the staircase they climb.

Essentially your players must feel that the purpose for them continuing on their journey with you is worthwhile. You will need to evaluate and reflect on your brand to see what aspects of it can best speak to your players to offer them meaning and purpose when they engage with you.

We'll explore this in much greater detail in Section 3, but to get you thinking on it now, we'll go through some of the gamification mechanics you can use to enhance purpose further.

When purpose succeeds

Purpose is a fantastic tool when it succeeds. An example of it 'in the wild' is the puzzle-solving game FoldIt developed by the University of Washington.

For those unfamiliar with FoldIt, it's a web-based puzzle-solving game. The puzzles that the player must solve are how to correctly fold protein-strands, hence FoldIt. Fortunately, there are only a certain number of ways proteins can fold correctly, thereby making it an accessible game for non-scientists.

Each newly found folded structure offers new answers for medical scientists to determine cures and solutions for a number of diseases, allowing for the development of targeted medicine for those diseases.

At least that's the layman's explanation. If you want a more scientific explanation, then we recommend visiting the FoldIt website and exploring it for yourself.

With each puzzle you solve, you will find yourself becoming engaged in the challenge itself but also in the good that it offers to humanity. FoldIt is one of the few examples that really connects to the concept of 'epic meaning', when a player engages with the platform. It is also authentic, and therefore people willingly give their time for free in order to be a part of it.

But don't be discouraged – not every organisation is out to save the world, after all. The lessons from FoldIt can equally be applied to an online retailer, an IT services company or any organisation. You just need to find the connection between your products and your customer's purpose.

Naturally, FoldIt also uses a great many other gamification mechanics and motivators to engage people. The underlying narrative is simple: solve puzzles and help save humanity. However, the basics of mastery (see the next chapter) are also present, as each puzzle becomes step by step more difficult than the last one, continually increasing both the sense of the player's purpose in aiding humanity and their ability to solve ever increasingly difficult challenges.

Hopefully, we've sold you on incorporating purpose, but how do you do it? What game mechanics can you use to instil purpose into your gamification solution?

Purpose game mechanics

Narrative & theme

The narrative is what you say about your organisation and how it relates to the player, while any recurring aspect of that story is the theme. Both are vital if you want to connect with your players.

For example, Innocent Drinks, a European beverages company, got its start by producing smoothies at festivals. It then went on to create a wide range of ethically sourced products, set up various charitable foundations and became a significant player in the recycling movement. It's a compelling story that doesn't really have a lot to do with the taste of its products, the thing you would usually associate with a drinks brand.

What Innocent Drinks have done, though, is build a compelling narrative around a specific theme – doing good. This theme is what attracted a lot of its loyal customers over its competition; they can probably find equally good smoothies elsewhere, but the brand's narrative fits their personal purpose.

Both narrative and theme, then, are strong mechanics when trying to build purpose into your tower.

When utilising these in your campaign, you need to ensure that the narrative you weave or the theme you choose aligns with your overall brand image and idea. It needs to be authentic to who you are and how you represent yourself. This should also be consistent over time – Innocent Drinks came under fire quite heavily twice when its customers perceived that it broke from its brand narrative, first when it partnered with McDonald's, and second when it sold 90 per cent of its business to The Coca-Cola Company.

A narrative and theme both create a framework, in which your player can immerse themselves and empathise with you, your brand and the experience you're designing for them.

That said, purpose, like a staircase, is not the sole motivator in a gamified environment. A tower with just a staircase is a pretty sparse tower. Purpose can be seen more as an amplifier for the other motivational levers – the higher you climb, the more engaged you are with every other element you find.

This is why the mechanic of narratives is linked with purpose because stories create context and understanding. Adding purpose, then, is an intentional action, but its effects are invisible, they are part of the background, the structure of the environment.

When using narrative as a mechanic within your business, you will need to take specific steps to ensure that a level of authenticity is indeed delivered to your players. You will need to identify whether the business or process you are gamifying already has a purpose to it. Revisit your mission statement to determine this. It is better to discover purpose organically and integrate this into your gamified experience, rather than adding one on as an afterthought, or one that is separate from your own.

For example, does your business save the Amazon from deforestation or is it trying to cure cancer? Both have a definite purpose that people can connect with; it wouldn't make much sense then to create a gamified environment based on another purpose.

But what if your business is a bit more straightforward, like selling paper and cardboard, or kitchen pots and pans? It still holds true that you need to determine what it is you want your players to feel. If you have a genuine purpose to your business, then integrate it into your gamification implementation from day one.

Don't make one up, though; players will see through this and will feel manipulated and drop off.

One crucial aspect that you must remember when adding purpose and using narrative is that it must always be done from the player's point of view, not your company's. Remember that the player is the Hero; they are the one on the journey; they will be accomplishing the tasks and defeating the challenges.

Your player will save the rainforest, cure cancer, create a bestseller on your paper or make award-winning meals with your pots and pans. Your gamified environment is merely the vehicle for this.

If the player doesn't agree or align with your brand's purpose, they will not be motivated to participate.

The power of stories in building purpose

The driving force behind almost any story is purpose, an epic meaning that is initiated by a call for purpose. Joseph Campbell, writer of *The Hero with a Thousand Faces*[44] (2012), is possibly the most noted individual for referencing narrative and purpose. A great many of the books, films and games that you and your players enjoy will most likely have some variation of Campbell's 'Hero's Journey'.

The Hero's Journey outlines the various stages that a Hero will travel through within a story. The Journey tends to consist of three parts: The Call, The Initiation and The Return:

1) The Call is where the Hero is called out of their ordinary world, given a life-changing quest and sent into the challenging world to complete this quest.

2) The Initiation is where the Hero must complete the challenges and ordeals set before him, something akin to the 12 labours of Hercules.

3) The Return sees the Hero accomplishing the final challenge and receiving their reward, which will either save them, save the world, bring them love, bring prosperity or all of the above.

We can recommend watching the original *Star Wars* trilogy to see the Hero's Journey in action.

It's worth mentioning that Campbell's research is based upon the stories that arise out of myths, legends and religions, which are strong creators of purpose in a great many people around the world through the ages.

One underlying requirement of the Hero's Journey is that the reader/viewer/player empathises with the hero, as they start out as an ordinary individual. This is vital, as you can't connect with an other-worldly being. But as the story progresses, the ordinary individual becomes extraordinary. It is the environment and the experience of the story that is offering purpose to the individual.

This development from ordinary to extraordinary is what all of us want to achieve, and is one of the reasons we all connect with stories.

Where can purpose fail?

The first pitfall is: **Inauthenticity**.

Being inauthentic to what you represent is a killer of motivation for your players. Think of the last time a famous fast food chain tried pushing their 'healthy' menu; did you buy into it or did you raise an eyebrow? This is the same for your brand; don't pretend to be something you're not. Your players will either immediately see you as a fraud, or they will be disappointed when they discover the truth.

The second pitfall is **Alignment**.

Don't expect players to align with your purpose automatically; every individual will have different values. You need to understand your players first and see if there is any alignment between their values and your organisation's (we cover this in detail in Section 3). Don't worry if you can't find anything, though; gamification doesn't require purpose, it simply enhances it.

The final pitfall linked to authenticity that we need to explore is **Choice**.

One of the most important concepts in any gamification process is the idea of voluntary choice. It is a critical concept in that you do not force players when using the purpose motivational lever. A player must always be given a choice to participate; otherwise, purpose does not exist. As mentioned, it is better if those choices also align with the player's beliefs and values. This is true even if there is an illusion of choice.

If purpose fails and you fall into one of the above pitfalls you can expect that your players will have one of three responses to it:

1) Drop-off
2) Compliance
3) Resistance

Drop-off is probably the least destructive and most common response from players. Drop-off occurs when a player is disinterested in the purpose behind your gamification solution and they decide to leave. You've lost a player, but they are no longer a negative influence on the game. An example is one of your customers simply not playing your game, or maybe not buying your product at this time.

While drop-off is a reasonably low-risk response, the other responses of compliance and resistance are much more dangerous. Edward Deci identified these two toxic responses in his book *Why We Do What We Do*. They occur when purpose is inauthentic, or choice is involuntary.

Compliance in our case is when players have lost interest, much like the drop-off state, but don't leave. They just stay on and go with the flow of the overarching narrative or trend.

If they decide to go with the flow, then minimal adverse effects occur, as they just won't engage with your experience. But this also means that nothing positive will happen due to this disengagement.

If they instead decide to follow the current trend of other player behaviours, then it may be that the players go along with more negative elements. Such as not caring whether other players or a community are unhelpful, or worse. This can then lead to the next point, Resistance, getting strengthened.

The last point, **Resistance**, is possibly the most destructive response. In our case, it is when the player(s) take an active stance against your experience. They feel and/or believe they have been cheated or tricked, or some other negative emotion, and now think that it is their duty to take their anger out on you.

If this was due to them being tricked, then they may have some just cause. However, if they are mistaken, then the best method to overcome this is to engage with your player community as a whole and discover where the issues lie so that the sense of resistance doesn't get out of hand and spread like wildfire.

These negative elements tend to happen in games that have marketed themselves inauthentically. Recent famous examples are often around games that have sold themselves as either free-to-play (f2p) or as an upfront single payment model – but then players discover that to enjoy the game as expected they have to continually pay through micro-transaction structures within the game.

In business, these negative elements often arise on social media. Brands with a strong narrative and a dedicated following are most at risk, with angry fans taking to social media to denounce the brands that they once loved to the whole world.

An example of this occurred in 2014, when Apple released its latest iPhone. Apple has one of the strongest brands on the planet, with a compelling story and theme that has developed over time and captivated millions. However, when it launched the iPhone 6, it celebrated the launch by forcing every customer to download U2's latest album. They unleashed a social media storm that lasted a very long time. They took away choice from their customers and acted in a way that many thought was a massive departure from the brand's narrative, and their customers punished them for it.

Summary: Chapter 7

Purpose is the underlying driver that pushes players along gamified systems.

It is linked to the narrative and theme that are both within the game but also that the organisation behind it represents (especially in marketing gamification). You need to ensure that you understand your own organisation's purpose, how it aligns with your player's purposes, and how to integrate this purpose into your gamified marketing.

Do this right, and your players will run up your gamification tower's staircases to reach whatever end goal you've placed at the top. Do this wrong and your players will at best leave, or at worst take up arms against you, often in a public way.

Next steps:

- What does your brand and organisation represent? What is your purpose? What is the story that explains that purpose? Why do you do what you do?
- When your customers come to you, what is it that they want? Think about the real benefit for the end user rather than the features of what you provide. How does this link to a higher purpose?
- Can you link the purpose behind what you do with your customers' purposes? Find as many links as you can, this is the core of what your gamified solution should represent and the story it should tell.

CHAPTER EIGHT

Building your tower – The gateways of Mastery

What is mastery in relation to gamification?

Our next motivational lever in gamification is mastery – the step-by-step progression and acquisition of skills that each person goes through in the pursuit of a goal, one that is often linked to a specific purpose.

'*Step-by-step progression*'…. So why did we use the metaphor of a staircase for purpose and not for mastery?

Gateways are a much stronger visual metaphor for mastery, especially when you consider the motivational influences that purpose and mastery each have.

The fact is, purpose motivates because it forces players to have a long-term goal, something to strive towards. Whereas mastery is not just a route towards an end goal, it is overcoming obstacles in the pursuit of that goal that makes mastery so motivating for a player.

Without these gateways, mastery would instead be replaced with mindless repetition of the same tasks with little to no growth or enjoyment.

An excellent example of gamification mastery is Duolingo[45].

Duolingo is an app and website that people use to learn a new language; an end goal shared by a vast number of people. The service takes the user through mini exercises based on a theme (like food, animals, objects), slowly building their vocabulary of words and phrases, then reinforcing them over time by introducing them in new contexts again and again.

Sounds familiar right?

This was/is the same method used in many schools when children first start to learn a new language, but like many students, the users can become bored and unmotivated by this rote-style of learning.

If this is all Duolingo was, it would fail. Much like the final French grades of those poor students.

The students would be learning with no explicit feedback of their progress or understanding of their skills over time. This would quickly become dull and demotivating for the majority of people. Luckily, Duolingo[46] knows this and has built mastery into its core product design.

Gatekeepers

One of Duolingo's main levers to encourage mastery is by blocking access to most of its lessons until a user completes prerequisite lessons or builds the required amount of 'experience' by completing language challenges at the current level of difficulty. This means you can't take the advanced food language module until you at least finish a basic module first.

By placing gatekeepers/tests between its content, Duolingo forces its users to prove their mastery over the previous lessons before continuing on to new ones. This creates a feeling of accomplishment for players as they progress and encourages them to continue with their learning journey.

Players are able to see their progress as Duolingo keeps a record of what sections are completed, and what areas still need to be unlocked.

Effective use of real-time feedback

Duolingo doesn't wait until the end of a course to give you a performance grade; it doesn't even wait until the end of a mini exercise! Each question you tackle gives you immediate feedback.

If you answer a question correctly, you get a big tick, and you move on to the next. If you are incorrect, the app shows you the correct answer and why you made a mistake, but it still continues on to the next question. When you get to the end of the exercise, the questions you got wrong are repeated to give you the chance to use what you have learned so far and cement your learnings.

When the exercise is complete, you receive the correct amount of 'experience', and the opportunity to retake the exercise if you want to improve your score even further.

This use of immediate feedback is a powerful motivational tool and is a key method to increase a player's mastery. Feedback is usually an outcome for performing specific actions, and while the reward/punishment of that outcome may be motivating in its own right, the knowledge of success or failure is often the most powerful motivator for the individual in their pursuit of mastery.

Any effective feedback loop enables players to build more successful strategies for how they approach situations, improving their competence at tasks, and their motivation to continue.

The Goldilocks rule of difficulty

As players get feedback over time, they will improve their mastery of the task until they no longer make mistakes. But what happens if you keep providing the same 'effective' feedback to your players?

Eventually, as players keep repeating the same exercises on Duolingo, they will naturally stop making the same mistakes. However, they will most likely have hit a mastery-ceiling, where repetition is no longer giving improvement, and this will quickly lead to the experience becoming dull – this is when players will begin to drop-off, as they find they are no longer being stretched.

Deci describes this situation well:

'The feeling of competence results when a person takes on and, in his or her own view, meets optimal challenges. Optimal challenge is a key

concept here. Being able to do something that is trivially easy does not lead to perceived competence, for the feeling of being effective occurs spontaneously only when one has worked towards accomplishment.[47]

This feeling of competence (mastery) is the motivating factor we are striving for. Challenges must be present that stretch an individual's skills and mastery; too easy and the challenge is no longer motivating, too hard and the challenge is seen as insurmountable and this in itself is also demotivating.

Lev Vygotsky termed this fine-line between levels of difficulty as the '*zone of proximal development*'[48] which is a vital element of ensuring that mastery remains a motivating factor for your players. Proper testing and evaluation are required among your users to make sure that the right level of difficulty is presented at the right time to keep motivation high; otherwise, you will inadvertently demotivate players instead.

Duolingo tackles this problem by asking new users to take an initial test of their current skill level. This evaluates the user's current knowledge of the language and places them at an appropriate point within the learning journey to ensure that there is a challenge and that they will be learning new vocabulary from that point forward.

What you can conclude from Duolingo, then, is that mastery is the growth of a skill an individual builds over time and practice while being involved with a (motivating) activity. Depending on the activity, this growth could be mostly unseen, but all mastery should be regularly tested, and this is where mastery's motivational power becomes effective at driving individuals forward, either to continue their successes or to overcome their failures.

Mastery game mechanics

How can you apply mastery's principles to your own marketing business? Here are three key game mechanics that are effective:

Quests and challenges

Mastery is motivating when players have a steady stream of achievable smaller, short-term obstacles to overcome.

Games often simulate this by including side quests and objectives for the players to complete as they progress – things such as killing a set number of monsters, travelling to a new location or solving a puzzle to open a locked door.

These smaller challenges are often bundled with learning new skills and used as part of tutorials and onboarding, helping players learn in a low-risk environment. As time goes on you can scale up the difficulty of these smaller challenges and force players to use several skills together to overcome them.

Start by thinking about what you want your players to do: create a profile on your website, sign up to a mailing list, read through your how-to guides?

Now think about what your players will want to master. If you work for a gym, your customers will want to master getting fit or losing weight. If you work for a marketing agency, your customer will want clearer messages and better Return on Investment (ROI) for their engagement with you.

You need to make sure that whatever challenges you create for your players to do and overcome, they actually match up with what your players want to master. Otherwise, your players will not be motivated, or worse, demotivated as they will see this as a transparent attempt to manipulate them into doing actions that have no value.

Using the example of a gym, a smart way to use mastery would be to incorporate training routines of varying difficulty, or chain-based challenges of attending the gym for X days/weeks in a row. This would be much more effective than marketing challenges we've seen in the past that focused on 'signing up for the gym's newsletter' or 'creating a profile on the gym's website'.

'But how does this help me?' Simple, by aligning what your organisation does with what your players want. By focusing on a player's mastery journey, you will motivate them to use your services and products more often. You can then incorporate more business-focused tasks like your website and newsletters as a secondary stream, one that can help them progress even further on their mastery goal. A great way to incorporate this would be to email players who are plateauing on their current challenge and remind them to sign up for relevant newsletters to get tips on how to beat that challenge.

Recording player achievements and progress

As we said before, mastery is a step-by-step progression each person goes through in the pursuit of a goal. What is important here is that on each step the player learns or grows in some way, and this is only possible through feedback.

One of the main game mechanics used to measure and represent progress is through points, specifically, experience points. As players do certain desired actions, they receive experience points. When players gain enough experience points, they 'level up'.

But is this linear track enough to motivate a player? Rarely. Successful use of experience points in games comes when it's used to determine a player's progression, and more importantly, what they have access to as a reward for their effort and mastery of the game.

In Duolingo, we saw that players gain experience in completing language modules and that they progress to the next set of modules once they had the required amount of experience. Duolingo would also show the player all of the modules they have completed, requiring the player to scroll and see their progress before continuing to the next module. This is a tremendous motivational lever for actually showing the player their journey and the mastery they've achieved.

Another example is airline reward points. The more you fly with your airline, the more 'experience' points you receive. When you hit a certain number of experience points, you level up to their next flyer tier. Different airlines work in different ways, but usually, each tier carries certain benefits like speedy boarding, free lounge access and access to special deals and upgrades. This is an interesting mix of the airlines rewarding their most active customers, while the customers actively work towards earning their deserved rewards.

Take a moment to think about what activities are relevant to your business. What would you reward players for and why? Make sure to keep this related to what the player wants to master.

Place big gatekeepers (bosses) in your player's way

The ultimate challenge for a player in a game is a 'boss-fight'. 'Boss' is the terminology used to describe events that push a player to the limits of their current skills and requires them to display mastery of the skill that they have been training in (or a combination of several skills).

'Bosses' should be significantly harder than standard quests and challenges. They are the rites of passage a player has to go through to prove their mastery.

Players should struggle to beat these boss challenges, but when they do, they should feel a sense of achievement and mastery due to the skill(s) they used to win. They should not feel it was a fluke or feel cheated in any way (especially if they lose!).

The most significant impact for players here is that they want to feel that they are improving using the above elements. Put a door in their way and they want to get past it – this is the key.

Going forward, a previous boss-level event may become a standard challenge for a player who has reached a higher level and is an excellent way to keep more experienced players engaged, and their skill sets fresh.

With Duolingo, this would be going through a language set and then being tested at the end to see if the player has mastered the required vocabulary to move to the next set. Only through regular usage and practice of the language over days and weeks can they master it. Then after the given amount of time/experience, they will have the opportunity to progress to the next 'level' of learning that language. Once they pass this test, what they've learned will most likely be a regular feature in the following sets.

Once a player does level up, there is usually a feeling of pride and accomplishment in the player; they will feel ready and more motivated to take on higher-level challenges. This is a powerful and proven system for motivating players and learners and can be easily applied to marketing and business scenarios too.

What 'Boss' challenges could apply to your business? How will you test your player's mastery?

Where can mastery fail?

Mastery is one game mechanic that is regularly picked up by businesses and used without thinking about the pitfalls that can occur when it is not applied correctly. There are three common errors you can make when applying mastery to your marketing gamification:

Unaligned motivations

I'm sure you have concrete goals and objectives for your marketing and sales teams, but these are unlikely to be the same goals and objectives as your customers and players.

When considering mastery, you need to think from the player's point of view and align your challenges, feedback loops and bosses around areas that your players care about. If you base all of your mastery challenges around your business goals or erroneous goals, your players will not engage.

For example, many retailers set up quests for their customers to sign up to their newsletters, create accounts on their websites or sign up for loyalty schemes. These quests reward players with occasional discounts and (usually) a lot of email spam!

But is this in the interest of the players? Many players immediately unsubscribe once they redeem their discounts and it's back to square one for the marketing team.

This is because goals are not aligned properly.

Instead, what if the retailer created a series of quests linked to certain life goals? For example, a kitchenware retailer creates questlines for players to buy specific cookware products to become a higher-level chef? As players purchase certain products, the company could send free recipes that use the equipment they have bought and reward them for completing the sets with additional discounts, recipes and maybe a 'boss' challenge?

The trick here is to try positioning newsletters, premium services and other business goals as add-ons and enhancements that allow the player to boost or speed up their mastery – not use them as the main event.

Challenges that are too easy

A common mistake when applying mastery in gamification is making the challenges too easy. Many businesses are afraid that if they make their challenges too hard, players will not engage. This is untrue.

You need to identify the various levels of mastery your players will go through and ensure that they progress through these levels at a suitable pace. Thorough testing is required, though, to ensure that your players do not become bored with the challenges you set them.

Bored players leave and rarely come back.

Many LMS (learning management systems) or online courses have this issue, where the final test at the end of their course is there as the illusion of a gateway. The player goes through the motions and passes with ease, wondering what the point of it was. No real mastery of skill or knowledge is tested, as the creators fear that if it's too hard, the players will not wish to continue and leave the course.

Challenges that are too hard

A less common mistake is making the game too hard. If players are not prepared for a challenge you set and they fail or do not receive enough feedback about why they failed, they will get stressed or annoyed and leave.

This is a similar issue to when a game is too easy; you need to ensure players are at the right level of difficulty for their current level of mastery. The best way to assess this is an initial test of competency that places a player at the correct point within your challenges, like the Duolingo example we discussed earlier.

Summary: Chapter 8

Purpose is the end goal for many players and the force that drives them through our gamification tower, mastery is the skills that allow them to do this. Mastery is the steady improvement of these skills and the frequent testing and feedback that helps the player grow and encourages them to keep going – just make sure you're helping them master skills that they care about and that are relevant to you too!

Mastery has two key balances that need to be kept in mind:

- **Difficulty**: Challenges can't be too hard or too easy, or your players will be frustrated. Constant checking is required to ensure your players are being tested just enough to keep them keen and continually improving.
- **Feedback**: We can't learn unless we know what we did right and wrong. Feedback gives this information but beware coddling your players with too much feedback; conversely, being too miserly and not teaching them anything will annoy them.

One last bit of advice – you need to make sure that challenges are interesting for the player. Don't be fooled into thinking that mastery is just a 10,000-hour grind – you need to make the challenge interesting and relevant to the player by adjusting the difficulty at the right points and providing feedback so they are always improving, not just doing the same thing again and again until they get bored and leave.

Next steps:

- Think back to you and your players' purposes. What skills do your customers need to reach the end goals of these purposes?
- Now think about your products and services. Do your customers need any skills to use them? Or do they help your customers with skills they use elsewhere?

CHAPTER NINE

Building your tower –
The passages of Autonomy

What is autonomy and how does it motivate?

The reason we've chosen the metaphor of passages for autonomy is quite simple; autonomy is fundamentally about choice.

Passages split off into different directions leading to even more passages and rooms. Your ability to choose which path you take and the availability of multiple paths is the crux of having autonomy.

For autonomy to be effective in any situation it needs two things:

- The perception of choice: does the player think they have a choice in this situation?
- The availability of choice: does the player actually have a choice in this situation?

If neither exist or are not well defined, the player will feel locked down and lacking freedom. This means that even if a player has a choice in a situation, if they perceive that they don't, they will feel restricted.

But choice is only one half of autonomy. The other half is the authority over how you make that choice and the time you take to make that choice.

Autonomy in an individual is:

- An authority over choice: does the player have the ability to make their own choice?
- The time for choice: does the player have sufficient time to make a choice?

Note, though, that when we say autonomy, we don't mean individualism.

Being autonomous in your choices does not mean isolating yourself from the choices of others. It just means having the means, ability and freedom to make your own decisions. Too often this mistake is made with companies and designers of gamification experiences.

In the corporate environment this idea of controlling your own time, and the ability to make your own choices, has resulted in a concept known as the results-only-work-environment or ROWE[49]. One of the most prominent examples using the idea of ROWE is the Australian company Atlassian.

Atlassian is a software company that specialises in collaborative software solutions for teams and groups in various business fields. What makes them so famous for promoting the concept of autonomy is not the software that they produce, but that they use ROWE to motivate their employees.

Each employee has the freedom, authority and the responsibility to manage their own time as they see fit to deliver the results required. This freedom of choice and ability fosters creativity, and this, as we know, is the core of the autonomy motivator.

Not only that, but they further stimulate this motivation with an activity which they have named ShipIt[50]. If ShipIt is unfamiliar, then you may have come across it in other literature as the FedEx Day[51], so named because company individuals are expected to deliver a solution, a hack, a new idea, anything within 24 hours.

The main concept of ShipIt is that once a year or once a quarter, every employee, from lowly programmer to CEO, is given 24 hours to pursue an idea that has absolutely nothing to do with their regular day job. And that's the main point; it should take them out from what they know to work with people they may not regularly work with, or at all, and come up with new, innovative, creative ideas that aid the company and its customers.

The reason that ShipIt is such a great example of autonomy is that the process starts with giving individuals the freedom to choose whatever they want to do. They then go off and brainstorm and find like-minded people across their companies to develop the idea and within 24 hours deliver it to be judged by their peers, not the managing board. This simple and fun idea has everything that a strong autonomy motivated experience needs.

Autonomy and gamification

Autonomy is the ability for players to explore their own creativity, to run with ideas that they organically generate, and most importantly, that they have a choice in what they do and how they do it. In practice, this means that they have (some) freedom to create and express themselves within an experience in a way that isn't entirely controlled by what the gamification designers have implemented into the experience.

Remember, though, that the experience will always have boundaries within it, and that as a designer you will need to place them, as total freedom creates a lack of direction. Even Atlassian's ShipIt has boundaries:

- The project cannot be part of the employee's day job.
- They must work with unfamiliar people.
- They must deliver it within 24 hours.
- And so on…

'When a user can continuously tap into their creativity and drive an almost limitless number of possibilities, the game designer no longer needs to constantly create new content to make things engaging.'[52]

What Yu-Kai Chou illustrates with the above statement is that the end goal that we want to achieve in any gamified experience is to set up an environment where the autonomy of the actions and the freedoms of the player will drive it forward without any additional interventions from the designers; a self-perpetuating loop of creativity and productivity.

Another example of where the autonomy motivational lever has succeeded is in the Health & Wellbeing application of Jane McGonigal's 'SuperBetter'[53]. SuperBetter builds a clear framework for you to operate in, allowing you to choose your own goals, challenges, rewards, etc....and allows you to determine how you achieve these various things.

You can use the application in any way you want to develop yourself, but if you are slightly lost or need guidance, it will offer you some suggestions. The freedom comfortably blends with enough boundaries that the player has a solid scaffold to attach their goals on to and to allow them the freedom of choice in whichever way they choose to achieve it. And in the end, they have an increased sense of self, health and wellbeing, better known as esteem, which we'll explore later.

Autonomy game mechanics

With a firm basis of what the autonomy motivational lever looks like and what it does to engage players, let's have a look at what mechanics you can implement when designing your own gamified experience.

Customisation

The very first thing that your players might see in your experience is the choice to enter their name and most likely create an 'avatar' that represents them.

This type of customisation is the initial point at which you can give your player autonomy and freedom of choice to choose what name they wish to have and what image they will be recognised with. Other examples are the player's team name and a team flag. Virtual versions are avatar names and what shape and appearance the avatar takes.

Avatar customisation is the most common example and type of customisation, but it is a very useful and subtle way of giving your players an initial freedom of choice. Being able to choose what your name is and what others will recognise you by is an empowering activity and one that has a significant amount of value for all players.

Customisation also increases the feeling of ownership over whatever decisions the player makes. The higher the sense of ownership in a player, the more value they will attribute it and therefore be less likely to abandon it: 'it's not just a faceless thing earning rewards, it's me!'

Although, naturally, the level of customisation you offer will be dependent on the type of experience you create, the aesthetic choices you've chosen and so forth.

If you want to delve deeper into the customisation experience within gamified experiences, then have a look at the concepts around 'mods'. Mods in games are generally community created customisations and variations upon the core experience. Modifications have a two-fold benefit:

- Firstly, they allow a player to customise beyond what you had initially intended, thereby securing their loyalty to your product or service even further.
- Secondly, the community is actively working together to further develop your product or service by modifying it. This would only happen if they valued it.

Allowing the possibility of modification of your product or service is one of the first steps in creating a state where creativity becomes a self-perpetuating cycle.

Exploration

Exploration is allowing your players the freedom to explore the gamified environment without restrictions, or more accurately, to allow them to explore without any apparent restrictions (this is because a game without any restrictions would mean creating an environment with nearly infinite possibilities, which is probably just a little bit beyond your budget!).

Depending on the experience you are creating, the environment could be a literal physical space, or it could be an abstract one, such as one that consists of knowledge rather than any physical elements or virtual representations.

Useful additions when using the exploration mechanic are to add the motivational levers of curiosity and surprise, by discovering and unlocking new information. Or adding small incentives for your players such as adding 'Easter eggs' to your environment.

Easter eggs are hidden rewards that the player only discovers if they choose to explore more remote areas or aspects of your experience and environment. These hidden items can contain anything, from additional information, to giving a bonus to the player or even as simple as adding a different colour scheme to an avatar. The list can be endless, but what it comes down to is that it is something that your player gets by not remaining on the 'prescribed' path.

The curiosity and surprise of finding something that no one else has found is a powerful motivator, and surprisingly engages a large variety of players.

Decisions

Decision-making is the action taken by the player once they have been presented with a number of choices. In gaming, the most common question is usually: How do we overcome this boss or puzzle?

The best games give their players multiple options to solve their problems. The players may not initially be aware that multiple options are available, but they will stay motivated as long as there is an implicit sense that if they keep trying they'll figure it out eventually.

This is a powerful engagement tool that motivates the player to keep playing, especially as they keep solving more problems this way.

This is because humans enjoy problem-solving, we practically live for it, and players will often attempt the same challenge over and over again to beat it in new and interesting ways. That is as long as they have the ability to and the freedom to approach it from different angles.

The pitfalls around multiple choices and decision-making have slightly heavier consequences:

1) First, the problem only has a few choices, and they are too similar, leading to very little experimentation and ultimately boredom.

2) Second, the problem is too easy; no experimentation occurs because it was solved on the first or second try. This again leads to boredom and likely drop-off.

3) Third, there are too many choices and this overwhelms or alienates the player.

4) Fourth, the problem is too difficult, there aren't enough choices, or the choices are not clear enough.

5) And finally, and this is especially true in gamified environments, the problem really only has one specific choice.

For example, with reference to point 5, say you are trying to teach a specific way to behave or to implement a procedure – as in the medical profession, extracting blood, or performing a scan or any number of procedures that have one specific way of doing this. The branching paths of choice and decision-making within a gamified version are then based around the skill sets they have learned and how they implement them in interdisciplinary and relatable activities elsewhere.

Where can autonomy fail?

Autonomy as a motivator is often misused and misunderstood in what it offers businesses. We've seen some of the pitfalls that occur within specific autonomy game mechanics but let's have a look at where the motivator could fail in its own right if misused.

The illusion of autonomy

The illusion of autonomy occurs when the choices given to the players have no meaning or value.

If people are presented with two products that are almost exactly the same, but the only difference is their names, then the choice is meaningless and valueless. An example of this can be when supermarkets sell the same product from the same source, but the upmarket supermarket sells for 20 per cent more than the discount supermarket. The only difference is the brand name, but the quality of the product is ultimately the same.

When this occurs, and the person discovers this, they will feel alienated and come to realise that the illusion was tricking them. The outcome of this realisation either on a conscious or subconscious level is that the person will fall into one of two categories: compliance or defiance.

Over-complicating choice

One pitfall that you as a designer must be aware of when creating environments to explore and offering choices to players, is not to make the choices too varied or numerous, as too many will overwhelm the player.

In most cases, the majority of people that enjoy exploring are happy with three or four options in a given scenario, as any more will likely overwhelm them.

A cautionary example from video games is *EVE Online*, when it first launched in 2003/04. The game offered a virtually infinite amount of choices and locations to explore when it was first released, and this is still a unique selling point.

However, *EVE Online* overwhelmed many players at its launch, as it unintentionally created a very steep onboarding experience that demotivated many casual gamers. A solution was to create a guided tutorial that initially limited the new player, but quickly opened up and allowed discovery over time at a pace that kept players interested.

This is a tricky balancing act to get right. Too much and you risk overwhelming, too little and you risk boredom. The only way to know for sure is to test.

Balancing the use of autonomy

When designing with autonomy in mind, an issue that often crops up is the balance between freedom and structure. If there are too many restrictions in place – like hand-holding the player through challenges and providing no choices – then you lose the benefits of autonomy.

When the player is no longer in control and freedom is an illusion, then we return to the first pitfall. However, if there is too little or no structure at all, then you don't have a game anymore, you only have a state of 'play'. This free-form experience could then take any shape, even ones that no longer have anything to do with what you had created. When your players are just 'playing' they are no longer working towards any type of structure or goal, and are unlikely to be doing the things you want for your organisation.

An example of this can be taken from the table-top role-playing world (*Dungeons & Dragons*, for example) where the facilitator softly guides the players to specific milestones in the narrative, and the players have complete freedom of autonomy to choose how they get to each milestone.

A bad example is where the facilitator has laid down such a specific path, commonly known as 'railroading', in which the players have no choice any more and are just along for the ride. Alternatively, if there is zero structure, and the facilitator has lost control, the players do whatever they want, never reaching the outcome and goal of the facilitator's gamified experience. It's the middle ground you're aiming for.

Autonomy and external systems

When creating such 'evergreen' structures, that encourage and incorporate autonomy, you must always be wary when attaching other systems to it.

In particular, beware of any system that adds an external value to it, such as a monetary value, or others that can have an element of needing to accrue an amount measured against the activity. With Atlassian's ShipIt, the only external value system attached to it is recognition and peer respect. The value that participants find in it is the participation and freedom to do something different and that others value it. In this case, we have a confluence of purpose and autonomy.

The issue with the external value system and autonomy is that the motivation behind autonomy is actively battling the external value system. Eventually, the external value system will lose its meaning, either because the individual no longer thinks that the value is worthwhile, or because it's too easy to accrue or because it doesn't reflect the input that they invested in it. Autonomy as a motivational lever should transcend this system, and the value should be internalised within the individual. The freedom to choose is what is valuable here.

As Pink mentions in his book *Drive*, autonomy in workplaces, areas that are driven by external value systems (like salaries), are and should be slowly moving away from the carrot & stick style of motivation. Just like at Atlassian and their concept of ROWE, individuals are more motivated by freedom and responsibility; the external value system is merely a recognition of that internal motivational value.

Summary: Chapter 9

Autonomy is the freedom you allow your players to have within your game; this fundamentally translates into how many choices you give your players and the freedom they have to make those choices. Care needs to be taken to ensure you don't overload your players, though; too many choices lead to overload!

By giving your players freedom, they will be motivated to explore the game you have created. This exploration can be funnelled into business outputs as players begin to understand more about the business.

Next steps:

- What choices do your customers make when interacting with your organisation?
- Are there any moments in your customers' journeys where they get choice paralysis?

CHAPTER TEN

Building your tower – The mirrors and windows of Esteem

What is esteem in relation to gamification?

Why mirrors and windows? We've chosen mirrors and windows because esteem is firstly about how players perceive themselves: the mirrors. But also how players are and want to be perceived by others: the windows.

Mirror, mirror on the wall

The mirror variant of esteem is about self-perception and is linked with the motivational levers of purpose and mastery.

A player's self-esteem is directly tied to their progress towards achieving their chosen purpose and increasing their mastery in that area. If a player feels that they are not progressing appropriately, then their esteem will decline or remain static.

Gamification techniques that give relevant feedback specifically on a player's mastery will provide them with internal validation of their skills and a boost to their esteem – increasing their motivation to continue.

Quantifiable feedback, like awards or badges, can have a significant effect when a player values them, as not only are they a reward for progress, but also a 'physical' reminder of this and their mastery, and each reminder acts as a boost for their internal esteem.

An example of this is in martial arts, specifically the belt grading system. As students progress in a martial art, they have to pass exams (mastery gateways) to demonstrate their skills. If they succeed, they are given a physical token that displays their new level. This belt is directly tied to their achievements and immediately boosts their self-esteem because it is a valued reward (feedback).

Windows to the soul

The windows variant of esteem is linked to external perceptions; what we want other people to think of us and what we believe they think of us.

People care about how they are perceived and recognised by others – the amount they care, though, is obviously a variable factor which is influenced by a specific situation, an individual's experience, values, upbringing, culture, and so forth.

The windows of esteem will cause players to act in certain ways to fit into roles they think they should be in. The more public a situation they are in, the more they want to affirm that role for themselves.

This means that a tower designed with 'windows' allows others to see how the player is progressing. For this to be effective, you need to incorporate gamification elements that quantify a player's progress and achievements in a way that is visible to others and meaningful for the player – and that is acknowledged and valued by a community.

If a player cares about a community and their place within it (see Chapter 11 on belonging), then they will be motivated to be recognised within it through these quantified measurements of their progress and achievements – driving them to perform actions that help raise them in the eyes of others.

Examples of this can be found in many running and diet apps that allow and encourage their users to promote their latest runs or weigh-ins on social media. This helps the user validate themselves publicly to their audience and boost their esteem, but also benefits the app which gets free marketing.

Depending on how you design your game, you can choose to limit the number of windows the player comes into contact with, by making private or solo experiences. Alternatively, you could also create a tower made entirely of glass where everything the player does is 'public'. Depending on your players and their esteem factors, you should decide where on this scale your game should sit, as it will have a dramatic impact on player motivation and performance.

We should note, though, that regardless of your decision of how many windows to include in your tower, the player always carries with them a personal 'mirror', even if you've not included any mirrors in your design.

Calculating the value of esteem

As mentioned, feedback is vital when trying to influence esteem as it helps the player understand that they are getting better at a particular task (mastery).

Quantifiable feedback like badges and trophies can be used to significantly improve esteem as long as they are valued by the player or the wider community.

Ensuring that you are providing high-value feedback is vital to improve esteem in your players and their motivation to continue specific activities that you are pushing them towards.

But how do you know what is valuable to players? Let's continue to use the example of a black belt in martial arts and explore what value this has:

Personal value (internal)

The student's perception of the value of the black belt will often be linked to how closely it is associated with their purpose – either the thing acts as proof of some milestone in their journey towards their purpose, or the thing itself will provide some aid in helping the player reach their purpose. For example, if the student's purpose is to get the top-tier belt, then the black belt is a significant milestone to achieving that (but probably won't be very useful practically in getting to the next stage – except for holding the student's trousers up!).

If a reward is unrelated to a player's purpose, then they will often not see it as personally valuable. For example, the student whose purpose it is to earn the top-tier belt will only care about receiving the black belt if they actually earned it, not if they just buy it off eBay.

Perceived value (external)

Perceived value is the value that another player or a whole community of players place on something. This value is often calculated based on the thing's rarity and cost/effort to obtain, although this can be skewed by social factors such as 'coolness', which is based on social norms and trends that heavily focus on belonging and social communities. The externally perceived value is often difficult to determine where players have multiple purposes and routes to mastery.

For example, a black belt will be highly prized by those of a lower belt rank who also want it and will be respected by those who already have it – but will have significantly less value outside the space with people who don't care about martial arts. This is especially relevant in gamification; don't expect people outside of your community to care about rewards as much as you do.

Actual value (balanced)

Interestingly, ownership often has a large distortionary effect on value. A person who owns an object will often value it differently than a person who does not own it when they are estimating its actual value.

The actual value of the object will be calculated based on this balance between personal value and perceived value.

In-game economies (or real-world equivalents) will often spring up if they are not included in games that have a focus on esteem and value, as players will want to trade things to aid their progress towards their purpose or stimulate this progress artificially. In our black belt example, the actual value of the belt is how much it cost the instructor to purchase it (you could potentially add the instructor's fees, too) – but this is unlikely to equal the perceived value.

Esteem and the value of feedback that contributes to it is fragile. This is because value is often calculated on the externally perceived recognition of feedback – upon which esteem is then based. These perceived values can quickly change between players or within a community – shattering a single player's esteem if it was based on this value. For this reason, we recommend designing towards multiple sources of feedback for players rather than relying on just one, and ensuring that players are building esteem based on personal value and not focusing solely on perceived value.

Esteem game mechanics

Esteem is essential to keep your players engaged; they need to feel they are progressing at the right pace and be rewarded with feedback when they do specific actions. Get this right, and your players will continually try to improve, get it wrong and they will do nothing.

How do you deliver esteem? Doing a quick search on Google for gamification will likely bring up two types of articles – one will explain the importance of points, badges and leaderboards, while the other will denounce them as the downfall of rookie designers. The fact is that both are right – points, badges and leaderboards are important feedback mechanisms used to portray a player's progress – but they are often misused.

Points

Points are a generic metric unit that can be used to measure anything you want; how many clicks a player makes on a website, how many words they write in an essay, how much money they spend on your products, and so on.

Points are a quick and easy way to provide feedback to your players. They do something right, give them a point! They do something wrong, take a point away!

Some of the most commonly used types of points in games that do exactly this are experience points (which represent a player's skill and mastery at the game) and in-game currency (rewards that players receive that can be traded for other things).

One of the clear benefits of points is that they are simple and easy to implement – think about what you want to incentivise players to do, and then reward players with points whenever they do it. Want your customers to write reviews of your products? Or to leave comments on your blog? Or maybe login every day of the week? You can give them points whenever they do these things and incentivise them to keep going.

An example of effective points is the discussion website Reddit and its karma system. Reddit's karma are points that are awarded to its users who post to the website – one post gives them one point. However, the system also gives all users the power to up/down-vote other users' posts, either adding or deducting additional karma points to that user.

As you can see, there is a clear method for gaining points on Reddit; these points have a conversion rate into their in-game currency (karma), but what are they used for? Nothing! This could be a negative issue for many gamified systems, but it works for Reddit. Reddit is an inclusive global online community whose members police themselves and their comments using the karma system. They are imaginary Internet points which cannot be traded, sold or used outside of Reddit – but have an incredibly high value to the users and the community as a whole.

So, points are a quick, easy win, right? Wrong. Too many designers implement points without a clear purpose. For example, a player leaves a comment on the company blog, and they get 10 points! Great! But what are these points for?

Many systems tend not to explain what points are for, why they accumulate, and what they can be used for. If points have no real function – either they are not tradeable, or their distribution is not aligned clearly with the player's purpose or mastery – they will not be a motivating influence on the player.

Another factor to consider is that points often lose value over time as players get more – too many games do not scale the usefulness of points as they go on, meaning they lose their impact and become redundant and annoying to players.

So how can you apply points to your marketing?

First, think about what are the small repeatable steps that your players will take when interacting with your game – writing words, leaving reviews, clicking on specific buttons, completing levels, beating bosses? These are the actions that you can potentially apply points to.

Next, work out what the points are for – will they be tradeable for in-game bonuses, will they allow the player to compare themselves to other players (see leaderboards), or will they be a marker for the player to show them how close they are to finishing the game (reaching full mastery or their end purpose)? In other words, do not make your points pointless!

Lastly, how will you introduce and explain points to players, how will you display them, will they be private or public, and how will you keep points relevant to the player over time as they increase in mastery?

The Starbucks Rewards marketing campaign is a great example of using points effectively by combining it with other game mechanics like customisation and progression. The Starbucks Rewards campaign could have been just a standard rewards scheme. If you bought products from Starbucks you would collect points; these points could then be exchanged for free items from their shops, such as drinks or food. This practice naturally fosters a minimum level of loyalty, as most people want to receive free stuff.

The difference in Starbucks' scheme is that they added progression levels, and each level offered different rewards. Frequent and/or loyal customers could even progress to a level where they could receive personalised rewards from Starbucks. This is ingenious as the customer is firstly invested in receiving the free gift, and through that joins an exclusive community loyal to Starbucks that now receives customised gifts that further increases their personal association to the brand.

Badges

Badges (and achievements) are usually visual/physical representations that depict the milestones that a player has reached on their journey in your game.

Unlike points, which are a frequent feedback mechanism used every time the player does a specific action, badges are more significant in that they are given once a certain threshold or achievement has been reached – for example hitting one million points, beating the first/last boss or completing the game in a certain amount of time.

Badges and achievements are common gamification elements because they are easy to implement and can have a quick impact on a player's motivational levels. They act as concrete, lasting reminders of past achievements for the player – showing them a history of the path they have walked towards their purpose or what they are still missing in order to complete it.

For example, in the boy scouts, which uses a system of badges to reward proven skills, getting a 'woodsman' badge proves mastery of being able to work with wood. The scouts are aware of what badges are available and what they need to do to earn them, and this pushes them to do certain things to get the missing badges and complete the set.

Another reason why badges are effective is that people inherently understand them. Anyone familiar with games or sports will automatically understand what badges or trophies are, meaning they require little onboarding or explanation.

However, this familiarity can also breed contempt – too many companies have already jumped on the gamification bandwagon and tried to blindly implement badges with no understanding of personal, perceived and actual value. These companies created badges and achievements that are disconnected from their players (e.g. badges for liking a Facebook page, badges for buying a product, etc.) and they do not understand why their badges are not motivating.

There are too many terrible examples of badges to name, but a good example of badges and achievements comes from eBay and their star awards.

As sellers receive positive feedback on eBay, they start to earn points and when the player earns a set amount of points they receive a star badge (yellow for 10, blue for 50, and so on) that is shown on their profile and sent to them as a physical certificate.

This is effective as eBay understands that customers want to know who they can trust on their website, and sellers want a way to show that they are trustworthy. These star badges incentivise both parties to engage with the eBay system because they align perfectly with what the users are aiming for – and not only that but getting an actually valued trophy for your service and being recognised by others as a valued user will have a lasting impact on the player's esteem and their motivation to continue.

So how can you apply badges to your marketing?

Think about what your players want to achieve with your business and map out the steps they are likely to take. At each significant point or hurdle consider whether a badge or achievement makes sense – would you be proud of it? Would you tell your friends or colleagues? This is usually the best test – if you can honestly answer yes to these questions, then include it.

Create a roadmap for these milestones and badges that are connected to your business objectives – but be warned, players will spot a marketing/monetary specific achievement a mile away and will avoid it or actively mock it.

Also, consider how these badges are displayed – do they appear when a player earns them and are never seen again? Do they appear in a player's inventory? Are they publicly visible? Do you show what achievements the player could earn? Do you show their completion rate? Will your achievements help the player in your game? Will they have an actual value, meaning they could be traded?

Leaderboards

If you implement points into a game, eventually players will start to compare their totals. This is where leaderboards come in.

Leaderboards can be motivating in theory, because players will compete with one another to get higher rankings, meaning they will be more motivated to perform actions that provide them with more points as they aim to improve their rank.

The trick, though, is to make sure it is obvious to players how they can increase their score, as well as why they want to do that. You need to make sure that leaderboards – like points – have a purpose, either because higher rankings mean better rewards (think about university league tables – higher ranked institutions will receive larger numbers of higher quality applicants), or because there is some pride or achievement in maintaining a certain rank (like beating your friends and getting top score on the local arcade machine).

The professional social media website LinkedIn uses leaderboards to show its users how many views their profile receives compared to their network. These leaderboards are not prominent – but they can be found when you look at your profile's stats.

On a platform where users are trying to network and be seen by others, this is a valuable insight and can drive users to engage more with the platform in an attempt to be seen more and drive themselves up in the rankings. LinkedIn has successfully identified a metric that can be used for their leaderboard that their users care about – even if there are no direct rewards for top rankings – and that encourages users to engage more with LinkedIn (which is clearly their goal).

LinkedIn's leaderboard approach is to provide relevant information to their users with no additional incentives. However, the classic example of gamified leaderboards in business is sales team leaderboards – where salespeople are ranked against each other to compete for salesperson of the week/month/year and win prizes or better commissions.

This type of leaderboard system is the one often used by companies first trying gamification for themselves; the problem with these types of systems is that they can lead to three types of behaviour:

- **The Chosen One:** A self-perpetuating loop takes hold, where the top salesperson remains at the top because they receive extra benefits for being at the top. This is very motivating for the top player but very demotivating for everyone else.
- **Cheating:** Gaming the system can be a big problem for leaderboard systems. If players are incentivised to score high, and there are no restrictions or checks against cheating, you should expect a proportion of players to try and game your system and score higher by means other than what you intended. From a game usage perspective this can be great, but what players are actually doing is not engaging with your game in a productive long-term way.
- **Elites v. Losers:** If top players have too much of a lead, it can be demotivating for other players who cannot see a way to bridge the gap. This is often the case with online games where the best players have reached unattainable levels for the average player. Games get through

this by adding tiers to their leaderboards so players can see closer competition and not be discouraged by upper tiers. LinkedIn does this well by comparing the user against their own localised connections and not globally – and improves on this by providing a snapshot of the users directly above and below them in the leaderboard to give an even closer idea of the competition and how to gain a rank.

So how can you apply leaderboards to your marketing?

First, you need to decide on whether a leaderboard is appropriate for you, is your points system robust enough? Can it be gamed? Do players care enough? If so, make sure the leaderboard is prominent, explained to players, and shows enough data to be motivating, but not enough to be intimidating. Consider showing what the player needs to do to improve their rank by 1, rather than showing how many points they are away from the top slot.

Where can esteem fail?

Incentivising the wrong things

Too many gamified systems focus their points, badges and leaderboards on factors that the business cares about, and not what the player cares about.

You need to focus on what the player will identify with as their purpose and the actions that will increase their mastery. The closer this alignment is, the more your gamified systems will motivate the player when they use them.

An example of poor incentivisation was with the taxi app Lyft. It offered the useful service of quick and easy taxi booking with credit card payment. After a period of time, it would then send an email of useful statistics about how often the user used the service and what ratings they received as a passenger. Lyft also had a badge system where it would award badges for travelling on certain days.

This all sounds nice, but people only use taxis when they need them. Very few people will order a taxi they don't need on a Tuesday, simply to get the Travel Tuesdays badge. The intrinsic value of the player conflicted with the (empty) value of the badge, meaning it wasn't motivating or a success for Lyft.

Under/overvaluing things

Knowing the correct value to place on actions and results is a difficult balancing act. If you overvalue a simple action that has limited business benefits and undervalue a more complex action that brings more business benefits – then you are heavily influencing players to act in a certain way.

For example, if you tell a player that for every 100 points they earn they get a free coffee, and you give them a point every time they open one of your emails – what do you think will happen? We'd guess you would get a lot of opened emails, but nobody would be reading them!

This can also be a downfall if players see inconsistency with how *you* value things versus how *they* value things. If a player sees that you are undervaluing something which they have a high personal value for, they are unlikely to be motivated to engage with you generally due to misalignment.

Removing player control

As we've discussed, esteem is directly linked with purpose and mastery; if a player feels they are improving, then they will feel better about themselves and compelled to continue.

But this can all go wrong if you remove the player's control during this process. A player will experience little personal esteem from any gains they make towards purpose and mastery if they feel like they didn't do it themselves.

For example, if you are using a language learning app like Duolingo to learn French and have been making slow but steady progress through the modules, you are likely to be upset and demotivated if your fluent speaking friend takes over and levels up your profile for you. Every time you now log in to the app you will see a fake set of your accomplishments and will probably be demotivated and disassociated from your progress.

To avoid this, make sure that whatever rewards a player receives are only earned through their direct actions. Not only that, but you should also steadily increase a player's autonomy as the game progresses to ensure that esteem can flourish.

Making the player feel stupid

Directly linked to a game's difficulty, if a player cannot beat a specific challenge you set, they will become frustrated with the game and likely lose personal esteem. They will not be motivated to continue unless they understand why they cannot beat a specific challenge and how they can beat it.

This is usually the fault of the game's designer for either making a game too easy/difficult at a certain point, or not providing enough player training to enable them to overcome the challenge.

Continuing our Duolingo example, a player's esteem would be damaged if they were started off on too difficult a module, especially if that module was labelled as 'easy'. You need to ensure that players only tackle challenges that they are capable of (or just capable) to keep them engaged.

Summary: Chapter 10

If purpose and mastery is the roadmap for a player, then esteem is the rocket-fuel that propels them along the route. Esteem is how we feel about ourselves and how we feel about how we are perceived. We are motivated by esteem to act in ways that make us feel valued (personally and by others) and will seek out feedback that helps us demonstrate this value.

Points are a useful game mechanic for esteem as they are a quick feedback mechanism that shows a player they are doing well at a certain activity. Badges are a more permanent version of points that a player can show off and attach value to, while leaderboards allow players to directly compare themselves to one another.

Just be sure that your points and badges have value to your players, otherwise they won't impact esteem!

Next steps:

- What do your customers value in regards to your service/products? And how does this reflect on them? Are you a 'status' brand, or do you enable or embody a specific lifestyle?
- What actions do your customers take that you want to reward and incentivise? What could you reward them with that would be of value to them?

CHAPTER ELEVEN

Building your tower – The chambers of Belonging

What is belonging in relation to gamification?

Belonging is every person's need and desire to seek out and build relationships or be part of a group of like-minded, complementary individuals.

Membership of a group will actively motivate people to perform specific actions to maintain their group status, either through group rules or through the player's own subconscious attempts to remain relevant to their new group-based identity.

People will often go so far as to alter their behaviour to fit in with the group's social norms. Imagine the new kid at school who suddenly takes an interest in the local sports team, because everyone else has that interest. They will gladly do what's needed to be able to take part in the social group that they wish to join.

Why do people choose to do this, despite the additional work required?

Remember we are a tribal species that flourished because of this natural trait – a group brings safety, multiple skill sets, division of labour, purpose, companionship – all a sense of belonging. The better you are at finding and maintaining groups, the more likely you are to survive and be successful.

In games, groups provide support mechanisms for players and can enable them to achieve much greater feats than if they were playing alone, either through direct teamwork, resource sharing, in-game advice or through emotional/psychological support.

Belonging is a strong motivational lever that many games and businesses often use, not only to recruit more customers but also to increase their customer engagement and loyalty.

But not every business and game do this right, and many overlook some fundamentals of belonging which lead to poor player recruitment, negative communities and high abandon rates.

Let's explore what the different factors and mechanics are with belonging, and what the key downfalls are if implemented incorrectly.

Wanted: Someone just like me

The belonging motivational lever can best be described as; the existence of, and the membership of a community or group that you can identify with.

Multiplayer games can quickly and organically develop these communities over time as long as players have ways of communicating with each other. These communication channels are vital because it lets players establish trust, but more importantly, it enables them to signal to each other who they are, and what they are about.

Each player will usually assess these groups and their members based on:

- **Demographics**: Location, proximity, language, gender, age, profession, ethnicity, religion and so on. Players may take some or all of these into account when evaluating other players and groups that are of interest to them. Depending on the situation, these factors may or may not be important, but note that location and proximity are usually a factor as it impacts when, where, and if players will meet.
- **Competence**: How good is the player at the game? What stage of the game is the player at? What skills/resources does the player have? The importance of these questions will depend on what type of player is asking them and where they are in your gamified experience. Some players look to become mentors to less skilled or inexperienced players, while

others may actively shun those who need their help and instead seek out their 'equals'. Regardless, most players will have a definite spectrum of competence that they are willing to engage with and will filter out anyone outside of what they are looking for.

- **Status**: Closely linked with competence, status is how the player is regarded by others. But it can also be linked to what group affiliations the player has, the history of the player and how active the player is at playing different aspects of the game. In other words, are they known by others, are they long-term members and do they regularly engage with the experience. Like competence, players will have a preference for a certain status that aligns with their expectations and will actively seek out or avoid other players based on this.
- **Goals**: What is the player ultimately trying to achieve? It could be as simple as playing the game for fun, but in a gamified process it could be that the player's goal is to develop a particular skill, save money, meet professionals in their field or pass a test that will help them get a promotion.

Of all of these, goals are the most critical factor when using the belonging motivational lever in a gamified experience. But why?

The impact of different demographics, competences and statuses will vary from player to player, meaning it is difficult to categorise them and make them appealing for broad player bases. Each player will have very individualised preferences which they probably can't articulate themselves. This makes it almost impossible for you to design a 'belonging strategy' around them.

Goals, however, are very different.

Most players can articulate what their goals are when playing a game – either the end goal of playing the game itself (to win, to have fun, to meet people), or the specific in-game, task-related goals (beat the boss, collect the points, pass the test) that they wish to achieve.

Even if a player is unable to articulate their end goals explicitly, their actions and choices along the way will speak for them. If a player's real end goal is to explore the in-game world fully, it will be fairly obvious based on their in-game behaviour.

It's for this reason that we recommend that you group players by their goals when designing a gamified process; this is the easiest way to do it and it's also how players connect with each other. We'll be exploring specific methods for grouping players in Chapter 14.

Three phases to belonging: seeking, building, comparing
Seeking phase: players are searching for a group to join

Seeking can be active and/or passive, usually a combination of both. Active seekers know they are looking for a group and will research and look for prospects both in-game and out of game (in the real world). These players have a much more concrete idea of what they want from a group, and who they are as a player.

An example of this is a player who knows that teams exist in a game, and who then actively reaches out to several teams to request an invite.

Passive seekers, on the other hand, are usually just playing the game and trying to reach their own goals in their own way. In the process of doing this, they will naturally come across others who share their goals and will likely end up as part of a group because of this.

An example of this is a player in a single-player game who goes online to look for hints at how to improve their score – over time they become active in an online forum that discusses the game.

Active or passive, players will often have an unconscious checklist (based on the demographic, competence, status and goal factors) of what they are looking for in a group and will be selective to make sure that whomever they approach is a good fit.

Building phase: players join a group

Once a player has joined a group, it then becomes a part of their identity. They will then (begin to) act in ways that reaffirm this to themselves and others.

This behaviour is often automatic as individuals take on group characteristics naturally over time and the individual's baseline for social norms becomes aligned with the group's.

The educator James Paul Gee speaks of this when individuals immerse themselves into the semiotic domain of an interest group (as the adopted group's terminology and methodology enter their own identity). This is an effective behavioural change tool that can encourage individuals to adopt other behaviours and attitudes over time in a non-intrusive way[54].

The real activity, however, in this stage is the upkeep of group membership. Different groups will have different requirements – some stated and some implied – that the individual must adhere to if they want to remain a member. This could be maintaining a certain level of activity within the game, paying a regular membership fee or being regularly active in the group's forum.

As you may realise, this is the sweet spot for motivation in belonging. If you have players joining groups that require them to perform actions that are beneficial to your business, then the self-regulatory nature of the group will encourage players to keep performing those actions. What we don't recommend, however, is trying to manipulate or create groups solely to get players to do this for you. Keep groups about the players and their goals; let the other benefits develop naturally as part of the group's dynamic.

Comparing phase: players develop a 'them versus us' mentality because of their group identity

This is semi-present from the start as players will filter out others who do not meet their internal checklists, but it becomes more pronounced when they are within a group.

A 'them versus us' mentality can be damaging for a game as it causes tensions between groups and can isolate players. However, it can also be a very positive motivating force that encourages groups to compete against each other and use your products and services more and in different ways.

The key to this is a balance; make sure to monitor communities and keep competition friendly.

You cannot eliminate this comparing phase; the very nature of belonging demands that players seek out others and form communities that will not include everyone. 'Them versus us' is therefore unavoidable.

Also keep in mind that while players can form groups within your game, they are likely to build or find communities outside of your game, too (especially if they cannot find what they want in-game).

Everyone has a strong need for belonging; once enough players are actively engaged with your game, groups will occur naturally – either within your game's ecosystem (company blog/forums) or elsewhere (social media, competitor forum, etc.).

Finally, it doesn't matter what kind of community it is, if a player is a part of a community associated with your game and it is satisfying their need for belonging, then they will be more loyal to you as a result (albeit as a by-product of their loyalty to the group). This will lessen your abandon and fall-off rates and helps to encourage your players to take specific actions.

Belonging game mechanics

Guilds and teams

Groups, guilds, clans, houses and teams are just one way of implementing spaces where players can connect more formally within a game. Different naming conventions exist for them, but all allow players to connect under a single banner officially.

Doing this provides players with a sense of inclusion, but only if the group aligns with the players' self-identity and goals. These groups encourage players to keep playing and to achieve larger goals beyond their solo abilities due to the sharing of information, resources and mutual support structures.

However, as with all the belonging game mechanics, groups can only work if there is player participation. A seemingly empty or inactive group is a sorry sight, and not many players will want to participate in them, causing them to leave the group and by extension, maybe even the whole game.

To combat this, you usually need to get the ball rolling and jump-start group participation with your own staff and a few specially chosen players whose goal is to build and lead these types of communities. This is where community roles come into play.

Tiered community roles

Community roles allow you to give different types of players different permissions. You can enable players to actively moderate groups by setting group rules – choosing who is, and isn't, allowed in, and rewards and punishments.

The community website Reddit does this well – each subreddit (a smaller focused group within the website) has a number of admins that can control every aspect of that group. These people are usually self-selected at first (because they tend to be the group's creators), but become community-selected over time, based on active users who show an interest in the role and who exemplify the group's ideals and rules.

This is an excellent motivational factor as admins feel ownership towards the groups they manage and are therefore dedicated users – but they also act as advocates for the group and are usually role models for new, and established, group members who will act in certain ways to please the admins.

Chat features

Chat features are tools that enable your players to communicate – through text, voice or visuals. This is often done through text chat, emotes, forums, comment systems and audio/video chat.

While many games either do not have these features, or have restricted them to an extent, players will tend to revert to out-of-game methods like social media or forums to communicate instead.

Communication is the primary method to form and strengthen connections and build greater meaning in relationships. We recommend that you consider adding the option of chat features to your game's ecosystem to allow players to communicate. These chat features can either be bespoke applications in your game or external applications (like forums) associated with your game.

Communication allows players to share knowledge, build trust and form connections. Sharing knowledge is a great benefit that enables players to learn from each other, improving their performance at the game – which subsequently enhances your business performance if the game's goals are aligned with the business's.

We do urge you that if you do use any communication features within your game, you also have sufficient ability to monitor them. Toxic players are unfortunately a fact of life, but regular disagreements and unpleasantness can occur even without their presence. Make sure that you are actively monitoring conversations where possible, and give your players the ability to report inappropriate behaviour.

While we recommend chat features as a fundamental building block for belonging, you should make sure that it adds value. Many games make the conscious decision not to include certain types of chat features; an excellent example of this is the team-based game *Heroes of the Storm*, which allows team members to chat with each other but blocks any communication between opposing teams. If you think that a communication channel will be abused, ignored or not add value to the player community – don't add it.

So how can you apply chat features to your marketing gamification?

You probably already have chat features enabled on your website through blog comments, forums, etc. However, these may be underutilised if you don't have an active community around your company.

The key is to understand what player groups you have – and then find ways to appeal to these customer/player types. Once you know how your players are divided up, you can create content specifically for them and target it specifically at them – this will be much more successful than the usual scattergun approach.

Remember, if your players aren't using your chat features – ask yourself: Why not? Do they add any value?

Voting and ranking

Not all content and communications are equal. Players know this and will value the community and each other based on their own interpretation of value. However, this value can often be difficult to estimate, and the ability to judge value can be distorted by those who 'shout the loudest and the longest'. This can cause a skewed impression of a community.

Players want to encourage, reward and/or punish each other based on the value of their actions. Giving players the ability to vote for or rank each other, or each other's actions, is a great way to enable this. It instantly quantifies the value of communication between players and encourages or discourages certain types of behaviour that the group deems appropriate or inappropriate. Not only that, but players who participate in voting/ranking feel more connected to the group and its future, strengthening their ties and ownership with the community.

While this behaviour can cement a group and its social norms, this may not be a good thing – destructive groups or players can emerge that actively seek to break this system. Elitism can also become a problem, with groups shunning new players who do not know 'the rules' and players seeking to play the voting system rather than the game you've designed.

So how can you apply voting and ranking to your marketing?

A good example of how voting is done right is with websites like Quora and StackExchange. These sites encourage users to submit questions to the broader community, the community then answers and can up/down vote each other based on the quality of their responses.

By enabling this type of mechanic in your own business, you can empower your players to moderate themselves and decide for themselves on what is valuable and what is not. This can come as a surprise to many business owners as they discover what their customers actually consider valuable communication.

We recommend using this mechanic primarily to allow your players to moderate each other, but you could also use it to let players vote on business decisions – what your next video will be about, what tech issue to prioritise, etc. You'll find that your customers will be more connected to you if you listen to them.

But be careful what you wish for! A famous example of this going wrong was Greenpeace allowing its members to submit and vote on names for a humpback whale they were trying to save – I don't think they expected 'Mr Splashy Pants' to win 78 per cent of the vote....

Exclusive v. inclusive communities

One last consideration when building groups is whether they are inclusive or exclusive.

Inclusive communities are open to anyone who wants to join, their membership is self-selected and usually based on how well the individual aligns with the group as it stands. These groups can organically change over time as members come and go, and different agendas and majorities take over. From a design perspective, inclusive communities require more moderation and monitoring due to this free flow of movement. It will take some more time and effort to ensure that they do not become negatively impacted by disruptive group members.

Exclusive communities are invite-only and are usually very focused groups, e.g. deeply invested, high-level players only. Membership of these groups can be a valuable status symbol to players and as such could have steep entry requirements to join, and high maintenance costs to stay. Ensure that the benefit to the group's members equals or exceeds these costs, since if they are aligned with your business needs they are a strong way to motivate players.

An example of both these community types is LinkedIn Groups. These groups are created by individuals on LinkedIn and can be closed (exclusive) or open (inclusive). There are many different types of groups, and they are usually themed, based on a particular interest type like social media experts, accountants, etc. The performance of these groups varies considerably based on the value each group's members place on their membership, which is often directly correlated to the quantity and quality of the content posted to the group. Exclusive groups often have the edge here as they can vet their members before entry and more easily ban members who do not keep to the group's rules.

So how can you apply groups to your marketing gamification?

You can implement this in your marketing gamification by grouping your players by goal type and setting up communities focused on those goals. Tell your customers about the relevant groups available to them and the benefits of being involved. Just make sure the groups are and remain active.

You can keep enhancing this further by creating content specifically for these different group types, and segmenting your messaging based on each group's goals.

Where can belonging fail?

Games that restrict too much communication

This can vary between games and players, but most players want to have the ability to communicate with each other in some way – especially if they can see each other in the game. We say *most* players because there will also be a sizeable chunk that will not want this – don't create two different experiences, though, just enable people to opt in/out of communication.

This is important as player needs are likely to change over time as they engage with different aspects of the experience, and the need for belonging is likely to kick in as time goes on. This is especially true in situations where knowledge transfer is required.

In most cases, overly restricting communication between players will likely result in them becoming frustrated and just finding out-of-game methods to communicate, e.g. social media. Ask yourself, where would you prefer the conversations to take place?

Games that do not support social growth

So, you've decided to enable groups, chat and the other mechanics we recommended. But nobody's talking…

This is the most common way belonging fails in gamified processes – organisations set up groups and expect players to jump in and start talking straight away and build a community like they have nothing better to do.

Your first step is to identify who your players are and what their goals are. Once you have this, you can then segment them into appropriate groups to ensure those player communities are focused on something that brings them value. See Chapter 14 for more on player identification and segmentation.

Your next step then is that you have to kick-start the conversations yourself – very few people want to be the first to speak and it takes a certain kind of person to start and grow a community from scratch with no real incentives. Over time, you will be able to step back from the community as it becomes self-sustaining.

It's better to focus your efforts on starting conversations around content that your players already engage with and start identifying key players who are more active and appreciate being given more responsibility for the community.

Games that do not address negative elements

'Don't feed the trolls' is a popular phrase online, meaning that you shouldn't engage with toxic elements of a community – it only makes them stronger and louder. This is fine for players to say, but as a game's owner, what do you do about toxic elements that could be scaring customers away?

Unfortunately, most game designers ignore them. This can quickly build to a PR disaster and lead to players abandoning both the game and your business.

The other end of the spectrum is banning players who engage in toxic behaviour; this can be effective when enforcing a zero-troll policy in your game but can result in the toxic elements resurfacing in gameplay, or third-party communities instead. On top of that, permanently banning players from your service also means losing a customer, potentially forever.

In the end, the middle of the road approach is what we advise. Some examples of this are to empower your players to report abusive behaviour or to empower your admins to issue temporary bans or other punishments (e.g. removing points). Allowing your player base to self-regulate through social norming adds value to the community and credence to what the consequences of an intervention would be. Make sure you monitor the situations, though, and have a clear policy on what would require direct intervention from your company and what form that intervention would take as well.

One creative example of dealing with trolls and negative behaviour comes from Blizzard's first-person shooter *Overwatch*. On top of empowering players to report abusive behaviour, Blizzard also set up a tool that automatically converted the most-used offensive phrases in the game into compliments about other players, or funny, self-deprecating messages about the player who had tried to be abusive.

Games that are too tightly controlled by inauthentic developers (breaks trust)

Belonging is a powerful motivator in keeping a community engaged with your brand and the gamification solution you created. However, it is easy to destroy, too. Authenticity and trust is a must in all communications and interventions with the community. If players suspect that you are intervening in their group for commercial reasons and not to improve their experience – they will leave. Or you cause an atmosphere of defiance or even rebellion. This can have even greater consequences, as a community that actively disagrees with your inauthentic choices can perhaps take it upon themselves to ruin your business. Examples of this can be found in games that have a strong community fan base, and then the company chooses to implement micro-transaction systems in them, to make more money out of the community. The community will often take up arms and ensure that the game is reviewed negatively on every social platform.

Such events can be very detrimental to your business and gamification solution. Be sure always to ask yourself whether your actions align with the expectations and values of your community.

Summary: Chapter 11

Belonging is a strong motivator that brings players together and builds their connection to your game. By basing player communities around their goals, you can quickly identify several player groups that you can build for and participate with. Encouraging communication between your players and empowering the most dedicated players will quickly ensure that your communities work and become self-sufficient.

Hopefully, you can imagine how this relates to affiliate marketing.

Next steps:

- What goals do your customers have when using your products and services? Are there any major themes or shared goals held by lots of players?
- Do your customers currently talk to each other about you or your competitors? Where do they talk? And what do they talk about?
- Are you likely to have any negative/toxic elements in a community you build? How would you respond to them? Imagine a few worst-case scenarios and the correct responses.

CHAPTER TWELVE

Building your tower – The parapets of safety and physiological needs

Value versus risk: the double-edged sword of safety in gamification

In our tower metaphor, safety and physiological needs are symbolised by parapets, and like any good tower, these parapets offer defence against external forces that could threaten our safety and needs. These defences can take the shape of avoiding loss, or conversely, conferring value on something worth defending.

To illustrate this dual nature between value and risk, we need only look at the mechanic of loot boxes within many commercial games. For those unfamiliar with the concept of loot boxes, they are a game-based version of slot machines that you can find in any casino. Even some of the visuals are similar between the two; spinning animations, lights and flashing symbols.

Loot boxes are meant to be a fun addition to games, where the player randomly receives a bonus by 'spinning the wheel'. However, depending on the game, the loot box can either be a fun free bonus for playing (getting a free spin every few levels), or it can be a bonus at a cost (like traditional pay-to-play slot machines). But like slot machines, it still affects our fundamental curiosity to see what happens.

This is because our brain is attuned to wanting and seeking (random) surprises, this is why we enjoy (and can become obsessed with) loot boxes and slot machines. But the secret behind the success of loot boxes is how they skew our sense of safety and physiological needs.

It is all about the statistical likelihood (and a sense of magical thinking). In other words, if only we had more loot boxes, our supposed statistical probability of getting that one item that helps boost our gameplay will be increased.

We can assume that the average player wants to maximise their gains and minimise their losses, and that they will use any method to achieve this. Within gamification, the safety and physiological needs motivational lever is the user maximising their value from your experience and avoiding any significant loss from engaging in it.

The trap that a system like loot boxes creates is that when the loot boxes are given a monetary value (pay to play), the need to maximise the value of the in-game experience is then inadequately offset by the financial loss that the player will experience by acquiring additional loot boxes.

In some cases, the loot from these boxes is purely cosmetic, but they do still have a cost. In that example then, it's an individual's choice whether to buy the box or not, as the only impact is whether you enjoy the look of the experience. Generally, this is a reasonably harmless use of the mechanic. Often the paid-for loot box is complemented by a free one given for playing the game.

The real issue with loot boxes arises when they become solely paid-for items that negatively influence the gameplay, not only for individuals but vicariously, for the entire community. Also, as many of the rewards in them are entirely random and unknown, adding a monetary value only exacerbates their inherent problems.

On the whole, people are likely to take a risk if they know what the expected value is and what the projected loss and consequence will be. A simple example of this is trying to jump over a river where the expected value is getting to the other side and continuing your journey. The known consequence is missing and falling into the river, and the known loss is therefore no longer having dry clothes. For many, this is an acceptable risk; you would likely get to the other side, but possibly not dry. However, the excitement and mystery of whether you make it across dry is still present. Therefore you would take the chance (probably).

The level of risk versus reward does depend on the individual player. Some will probably read that parable and say 'well I'd spend the extra time and find a bridge', in which case their loss/risk aversion is higher than the person who would take the leap and see what happened. Neither is wrong, and neither is right. But what these randomised mechanics do in us is alter our perception of our own personal loss/risk aversion values. Depending on the environment and the situation, many would be swayed to take higher risks than possibly needed. It depends on the imagined reward and how much we want/need it.

The benefit, though, of adding a loot box-like mechanic over the slot machine variant, is that with loot boxes there is always a guaranteed reward. It may not always be a reward that your player wants, but at least they get something. With a slot machine, they will spend 99 per cent of their time/money and get nothing back (the actual numbers are different, but for ease and simplicity we'll go with these). The knowledge that you always get something from a loot box is why this mechanic is so useful for pushing people outside their natural safety zones.

To strengthen this mechanic even further, you as a designer can layer it with other complementary mechanics, such as the 'Fear Of Missing Out' tool, or FOMO.

For those unaware, it's essentially the sensation that unless the individual participates, they will lose out on knowledge or miss out on receiving some unknown but essential experience. This awareness of missing out creates a motivating sense of agency in the player to take part in the experience. All of this is based on a perceived value that they have personally attributed to the experience, based on the level of the perceived loss that they may experience if they fail to take part.

Perceived value

Perceived value is an important aspect of the safety & needs motivational lever. Although it is the individual who places the perceived value on something, the perception is informed and affected by the knowledge they have gained from external information, like a community. And how a community would determine the value of something is also determined through a few methods.

One such method is through the use of scarcity. Scarcity usually isn't seen as a positive, as it generally drives unwanted behaviours and negative emotions. However, used correctly, scarcity can strengthen a healthy want/need, and it can attribute a perceived value that is above the actual value of an object or experience. If we take the example of loot boxes, on the one hand the scarcity of an item can create an unhealthy obsession with a game, on the other, scarcity of an item to unlock something can create a strong loyalty to the game. Depending on your end goals, if it's to aid and improve an individual's experience, then using scarcity can actually help both you and your user.

The psychological effect from such a method is the concept of a 'Sunk Cost Dilemma'. This is where the player will place a far higher value on what they own or have experienced, due to the time and effort they have placed on the activity of acquiring the item or knowledge. What this creates is a safety zone that the player wishes to defend and avoid losing. As Yu-Kai Chou puts it: '(...) *Loss & Avoidance sometimes manifests itself through our refusal to give up and admit that everything we have done up to this point has been rendered useless*.'[55]

This sentiment is echoed by Daniel Kahneman and his concept of the two systems in our psyche. This explains a situation where the current active system, System 1, is battling with the backup system, System 2, which refuses and avoids accepting a change in historical experience, for example, a change in value that doesn't fit into the current paradigm of the player's mind[56]. This could take the shape of refusing to accept that spending money on a (bad) loot box system is actually damaging, because the hours spent accruing the loot boxes needs to have some value. Otherwise the loss is too emotionally damaging.

Randomness and transparency

It is the randomness of loot boxes that leads to obsessive behaviour (as you can see in gambling). The chance of whether it'll be a win or a loss is what grabs everyone. And yes, we do mean everyone.

No one is exempt from this, only the depth of the obsession differs between people. We as designers must always be aware of this effect when creating gamified experiences. As the random surprise mechanic of winning or losing is extremely appealing, it should therefore only aid, preferably over the short term, in strengthening a commitment to the desired action, and not become the reason for the action in and of itself. Otherwise, we've created another slot machine that people cannot escape, and that is neither sustainable for the player, nor for the designer in the long term.

To support us as designers in avoiding such an outcome, we must remember to remain transparent, specifically with the transparency of possible outcomes concerning loss or gain. Negative emotions and reactions will occur for the player when a loss is experienced for an unknown or unexpected reason. If there is no transparency in the reasoning or in the possible outcomes, then the players sense a lack of choice, and this removes agency for them as they will believe that there is no way to alter this negative outcome, or no alternative choice.

Abundance and scarcity of choice

When dealing with a sense of safety, needs and choice we need to consider the delicate interplay between the abundance and scarcity of the choices we offer players. Players must at the same time be aware that they have choices but also be unaware of what those choices entail.

To borrow a concept from Peter Schwartz, 'Emergent Complexity' is a methodology of behaviour in which optimal amounts of choice can be added into an experience so that the player is continually challenged.[57]

For example, when we take a look at Maslow's Hierarchy of Needs each stage has prerequisites (Figure 4). As we complete challenges in each tier, we are offered new choices and challenges in the next tier. And each one has its own responsibilities and consequences. They are also, at this point in time, transparent to us. Emergent complexity is

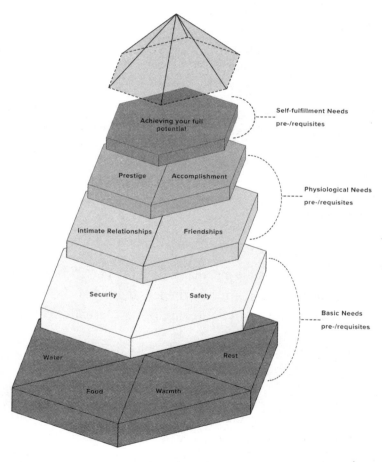

Figure 4.

just that, each step taken builds upon prior experience and increases the challenge in the next. Too much at once would paralyse the player. A slow progression of gradually increasing choices and challenges is, in fact, empowering to players.

The opposite, then, is too much scarcity of choice for players. Offering too few choices to the players disempowers them, which if the difficulty of the challenges is too high, leaves them with no alternatives; thus lowering their sense of safety and comfort in the activity that they are taking part in. The right balance must be found, so that the level of scarcity is just enough to challenge them with the right level of difficulty so that it increases their engagement with the experience and also offers a level of replayability for them. This is because many will want to try a difficult task again and again to refine their skills and abilities.

Once you hit this balance, you have found what Lev Vygotsky named the *zone of proximal development*[58] (Figure 5), and within that, your players will find what Mihaly Csikszentmihalyi has called

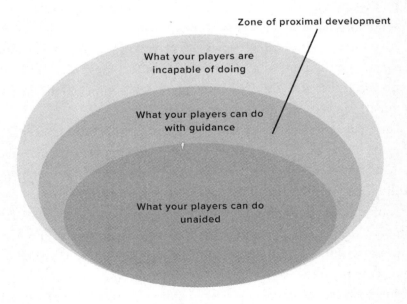

Figure 5.

'*Flow*'[59] – the moment where the player's ability almost matches the level of challenge presented to them, and they overcome it, moving on to the next challenge. The essence of the motivator behind safety and physiological needs is bringing all of these together, so that the player's safety and needs are challenged and disrupted enough. They then rise to the occasion and extend their ability to reframe themselves and expand what they previously would have considered their comfort zone.

Safety & needs game mechanics

But if these needs are so powerful, what mechanics can we use to effectively (and safely) pull the motivational levers of safety and needs within your players? Let's delve a little further and see what options are available to you.

Time-dependent rewards

Time-dependent rewards, opportunities and consequences are a common mechanic and are easy to implement.

They appear as countdown timers for players to take a specific action, like getting a discount or a larger prize than they normally would for completing an action. This makes the player feel compelled to take part in something because time is running out.

Time-dependent rewards work well with the FOMO concept, as when the timer runs out the reward is gone. Bidding systems, like eBay, use countdown timers like this, which at times will cause a frenzied bidding war near the end of the sale. This is part of eBay's fun.

Countdowns are also useful in increasing the perceived value of an item and to increase the engagement of those interested in the item. Continuing our eBay example, many items are sold for more when bid upon, compared to just listing the item for a specific price.

However, use this mechanic with caution; if it is used too flippantly or too strictly the players will either have an unhealthy obsession with it or burnout from it. This is the case when players see many time-dependent rewards but cannot action them because they are time poor, or the reverse, they spend too much time chasing these actions and get bored with the game too quickly.

One example that uses time-dependent rewards, but is a repeating event, is any national lottery game, as the player is given a new chance every week to buy the ticket before time runs out to get the reward. It's an effective system because it generally has a low-cost and low-action buy-in. It doesn't take very long to take part, a few minutes, and has a low monetary cost. Because of this low barrier to entry, people return to play again and again. If these barriers to entry were higher, then the time dependence would turn people away from it eventually.

Randomised rewards, punishments, events

Randomness as a mechanic can directly affect the sense of safety and needs in players. Nothing is more exciting and anxiety-inducing than something random and uncontrollable. But with random rewards, we need to also consider random consequences, punishments and events.

When you use consequences or punishments, do not veer so far into the negative motivational area that the player becomes withdrawn from your experience. Use punishments as a final resort and only in an area where your players are resilient enough and that the act of punishing is sparse. Consequences, on the other hand, are very useful, as they can be very motivating when used correctly. Consequences are everywhere, the time-dependent mechanic has built-in consequences, FOMO is a consequence. A consequence is, in this case, a more severe outcome that has enough emotional weight so that it pushes and motivates a player to engage in the way that you wish them to.

As before, though, do try to use these sparingly, as an experience that has too many pseudo-negative outcomes will eventually push your players away and effectively estrange them from what you wish to have them engage with.

Safety & needs case study: _LootCrate_[60]

An example of a product/service that utilises pure mystery, curiosity and discovery is the company LootCrate. It is a subscription-based service, where once a month you are sent a box of items, usually any paraphernalia associated with geek or pop-culture. The hook of this service is that the contents are completely unknown, you never know what you are going to get.

A prospective customer can go on their website and see what the general genres are or what previous months have contained and get their interests piqued, but that only gives them a general insight into the possibilities.

And thanks to the subculture of 'unboxing' videos on sites such as YouTube, LootCrate has got an even larger following and broader interest in its model. Using images themselves and their broader community to create visual marketing, they have grabbed the curiosity of many more people. People 'need to know' what's in the next box, and the only way they can do it is by paying for the monthly subscription.

All the contents are mostly things they want, to some degree, so there is no real sense of loss or alienation in the people that receive the items. They are generally satisfied with what they have been given. Even though it's a surprise, most people generally have an idea of what to expect.

Limited life rafts

Life rafts are a tool that allow players to continue beyond, or survive, a challenge that would otherwise beat them. They are small 'get out of jail free' cards that help players in their time of need.

All of us will have seen life rafts used somewhere on TV game shows like _Who Wants to Be a Millionaire?_ or _Deal or No Deal._ Game shows provide these life rafts to help players in situations where their skills aren't enough to continue, but they limit the quantity or effectiveness of the life rafts in some way to keep the player (and the audience) engaged.

A good example of this is with *Who Wants to Be a Millionaire?* It gives each player three life rafts: ask the audience, phone a friend or 50/50. Each life raft can potentially make answering the problematic question easier, but can still prove ineffective if the audience gets it wrong, or the friend they phone doesn't have a clue.

Once the life raft is used, many games stop it from being used again – either completely, for a length of time or until a player does something to earn it back.

Remember, life rafts are meant to help a player in a moment of need, but not to give them a free pass. Free passes tend to break engagement with a game, as players would cease to grow in mastery and would lose esteem over time as they relied on the life raft.

Another more sinister way is using life rafts as breadcrumbs. The player, at certain points in the experience, is being purposefully blocked by an external force and the only way to move on is with the life raft. The life raft is now compulsory and no longer optional as in the previous case. The player thus feels compelled to use it, because they want to continue. The player will eventually experience burnout from this mechanic, especially when it costs money.

Many 'free' mobile game companies use this method. After the player works their way through so many levels they eventually come across one they cannot beat (a rigged level). They find the only real way to get around it is to use (an often paid) life raft, after which, the levels get easier again until the next 'rigged' level.

Easter eggs

Easter eggs are self-explanatory, but for those unfamiliar, an Easter egg is an unknown, random, but welcome surprise for a player. As with an

Easter egg hunt, you don't know where they are (if there are any at all), but if you find the egg, you're pleased that you did.

Many games and gamified experiences use them. These Easter eggs are usually in-game secrets, extra information, hidden challenges or rewards and are hard to find.

The best example of Easter egg usage is within the practice of the Alternate Reality Game (ARGs) genre, which straddles the area between a game and a gamified experience. ARGs are usually an immersive puzzle game that spans across the real and digital worlds, making players solve puzzles to progress.

One example of an ARG is *HiddenCity*[61], a puzzle-solving game that requires players to solve clues that are texted to their phone, that they can only solve by exploring famous landmarks in their city. Each clue makes the player travel to a new area and explore for the Easter eggs in that area to solve the puzzle. When they do, they are then sent the next puzzle to solve.

Other games and gamified experiences use Easter eggs as bonus rewards for players who go the extra mile. For example, in an exploration game, if the player purposefully goes off the beaten track and takes the extra time away from the primary objective, you may reward them with an Easter egg that holds an exploration bonus.

Easter eggs are effective as they surprise players and reward them for exploring and investing time and energy into your game. Players feel vindicated for their actions and are more motivated to continue.

Where can safety & needs fail?

The main failing of using these mechanics is the possibility of creating an 'addictive' or wholly absorbing experience.

Some may believe that this is the desired outcome because full absorption means total engagement with the experience (a player is utterly obsessed with your product or service), and yes, in the short term, this can be useful/profitable. However, in the long run, it will lead to burnout and is effectively you failing the customer. What you have created then is a customer experience that leaves the player depleted, an empty husk essentially that is harmful in the long run – eventually losing you customers and gaining you a negative reputation.

A huge amount of 'free' mobile games are great examples of this. They feature quick, easy wins with no intrinsic value in them. They burn through their entire customer base with 'addictive' game mechanics until eventually they run out of customers and move on to the next thing. Other examples are any that have to do with gambling and its totally absorbing properties.

Gambling leads on to the next failure in usage, and that is having experiences where the risk is too high, and the outcomes or consequences are (un-)intentionally negative.

Be aware that this is different from a weighted consequence as discussed earlier. In this case, if the risk is too high, then the outcome can have long-lasting adverse effects on an individual's life. In the example of gambling, it is someone who enters a high-stakes poker game without understanding the risks and consequences associated with it. This naturally links back to educating your players and being transparent with them about what the outcomes are.

Our final word of warning when using mechanics based around safety and needs comes when you employ tools that accentuate rarity, scarcity and exclusivity. The majority of endgame content and experiences are based around these three concepts, as you want only the most loyal of players to get them.

If everyone got the exclusive content, then it would defeat the point of a journey, though you must make sure that the exclusivity, rarity and scarcity is not so random or hard to get that it alienates your players, as with the loot box examples or with content that requires so much repetitive behaviour to get the 0.01 per cent drop rate to occur, as with many massively multiplayer online role-playing games or MMORPGs (like the popular game, *World of Warcraft*).

JetBlue[62] is a good case study example of where both sides of the coin happened; they created a very useful frequent flyer loyalty programme that had exclusive rewards for its most loyal customers. Unfortunately, its discovery and onboarding phase required too much effort and too much private information, thus lowering their sign-on base, and some of their endgame rewards were one-time rewards for those select few that got to them first. This regrettably led to a fall-off in their customer loyalty, despite initially using some effective mechanics.

Summary: Chapter 12

Using the motivational level of safety & needs is a delicate balancing act where the player is weighing up the possible values, risks, consequences and outcomes of actions they need to take within your experience. Giving them limited choices while leveraging mechanics such as FOMO, life rafts and Easter eggs can increase their motivation and sense of agency, but it can also cause them to become obsessed with trying to gain more or estrange them from the experience entirely.

Next steps:

- Consider which mechanics work well with your business values and goals. Consider whether these create a healthy player engagement or cause a negative obsession.
- Which mechanics work best within your campaign and how much transparency are you able to give without giving up the surprise?

SECTION THREE

Actions

Now that you've gathered all the pieces and resources for your very own tower let's move on to the next step of actually building a gamification tower.

This section is a practical, step-by-step guide to building your own effective gamification tower.

What you will be learning in the coming chapters is how to determine who your user base and target audience are, what possible problems could arise, how to measure your gamification campaign and how to build your 'ideal' gamified tower.

But don't worry, we won't just tell you what to do and leave it at that. The way we're going to guide you through the gamification tower framework is by using a fictional business as a case study, so you have an example you can compare against that grows with every chapter.

The Thunder Gym – a gamification tower example

The Thunder Gym is a made-up organisation that we will use in each chapter going forward so you can see how we build a gamification tower from the ground up. We will use other case studies and examples throughout as well, though, so that you can see how to apply the learnings to your own business.

There are two reasons for using the gym example. One, everyone understands what a gym is so there should be little confusion around what we're talking about. And two, while gamification marketing can be applied to any organisation, it is most effective in a service-based business like a gym where customer engagement is one of the main priorities for marketers.

The Thunder Gym case study will be the red thread throughout this section, tying together the various concepts and theories into a coherent linear narrative. It will use the viewpoint of a new marketing executive within the gym, making all the relevant decisions.

Jumping in

For those of you anxious to get started and jump right into building your own gamified experience, we'll give you a quick rundown of how best to use this section in conjunction with the rest of the book – and in case any of you decided to jump right up to this point after the book's introduction.

We've designed this section to build upon knowledge in a step-by-step manner. Chapter 16 is the actual guide of how to build your tower – the various stages needed to have an effective gamified experience. It will use the various floors and motivational levers that you learned about in the previous section.

The other chapters will lead on to and augment Chapter 16 by helping you discover and learn about who you are and what it is you wish to get across to the player. What the problems are that you are trying to solve by offering the gamified experience to your players, who your players are and how to identify them and offer the correct experience. What the pitfalls and problems are that may occur once you have built your tower, and finally how to measure the outcomes of your experience.

We're going to refrain from saying how to measure success and failure, because you'll likely fail, a lot, at the beginning, which is good. As long as nothing breaks you can learn from it, you can iterate and improve upon your designs. We'll take you through this in the final chapter, and each piece of information will get you and your players closer to a memorable and meaningful experience. So, enjoy and have fun!

CHAPTER THIRTEEN

Who are you?

Welcome to *The Thunder Gym*!

In this section of the book, we're going to pretend you are the new marketing executive at this fictional gym. You've been brought in to work on the company's marketing as a whole, but your specific focus is on new customer acquisition and improving current customer engagement.

Your new manager (the owner) has heard a bit about gamification and wants you to design a gamification solution for the gym and to then sell your idea to them, but has no idea where to start. They wave their hands dismissively and tell you to work something out.

Luckily, you have this book to guide you. But where to start?

A quick note before we begin:

As you go through this process, you should keep in mind an important consideration, which is whether the leadership and key internal stakeholders of your organisation are interested in gamification. This is because before you even sell your new experience to consumers, you need to sell the project internally to the owners and the stakeholders. Without their support, it will not only be a monumental task to create, but it may also end up being a futile one. We'll cover this later on, but be mindful at this early stage.

The company

As the new marketer, your first step should be to explore and analyse 'who you are' as an organisation. This is often linked to why the organisation exists in the first place, its history and its current situation.

You should interview the relevant people in your organisation and find out the following to start with:

- Organisational background
- Products and services offered
- Team structure and resources

Organisational background

You need to explore why the organisation was created in the first place – what problem does it solve and for whom? This will take you all the way back to the founding of the organisation, and you should work your way forwards from there to get a good understanding of where it is now, and the decisions made that led it there. Importantly, you should also find out what its plans are for the future, too.

For *The Thunder Gym,* after a briefing from the gym owner, what you understand so far is that it was founded to provide an approachable gym experience for the everyman, the average Joe – people who were too nervous about going to professional gyms or priced out of expensive spas. *The Thunder Gym* gets most of its customers from the local towns, and it has no aims yet to become a global franchise. But that doesn't mean it's a small enterprise; it's still a capable gym that can service a few hundred people every day. Its main problem is that it still isn't at capacity yet and is struggling to find new, active customers in the local area.

So far we've established a few starting points for the gym, what its capabilities are and what its immediate aims are. This is important because you want to make sure that you create marketing goals that are in line with the overall business. There would be no point in creating a plan that aims to make *The Thunder Gym* an international phenomenon if the business isn't looking to support that kind of customer or strategy.

Products and services offered

Next, identify all of the products and services the organisation offers, then for each product/service, identify the following:

- What pain point does this address for the consumer – what problem does it solve?
- How does the organisation perceive this internally – is it a good product?
- Where does this product sit in its life cycle – has it just been launched or is it winding down?
- What can be done to improve the product – is gamification an option for it?
- Why does the organisation offer this product/service?
- How are the products/services delivered – is it a digital product or a face-to-face service?
- What is the total experience of using each product/service from start to finish?

You should also work out how each product/service fits into the overall portfolio of the organisation. A useful tool for answering these various points is the Boston Consulting Group's matrix for identifying which products and capabilities are core to your company and which require improvement or change[63]. This simple tool should help you quickly identify which products/services to focus on by charting its position on a graph of relative market share v. the market's growth rate.

Team structure and resources

Once you've established the overall background and aims of your organisation and the products/services it offers, the next step is to look at what resources are at your disposal. Resources include the people you have access to and their skills, but also the budget you have to run a gamification project.

You should consider the following:

- Is there a set-aside budget for the gamification project? This is both for time and financial budgets.
- Do you have access to specialist internal skills like programmers, designers, UX testers, etc.?
- Does anyone on the team have any experience with gamification?
- What is the wider team's attitude to this type of project – supportive, apprehensive, hostile?
- What is the wider team's expectations of the outcomes of this project? Consider their expectations not only of results but of the deliverable itself (are they expecting an app when you deliver a physical card-based loyalty scheme?)

Depending on these capabilities, the route you take with your gamified solution may vary considerably. For example, does your company have coders for an app-based solution, or is it more face-to-face oriented with direct interaction and coaching? You can only deliver within the scope of the resources you have, so be sure to keep your aspirations grounded in this reality.

Where do you fit?

Once you have a solid understanding of your organisation and its products, you next need to identify where you fit into your industry and the world. Not having a broad understanding of this will cause issues later on, as you may create something that already exists, has failed before or just won't work.

To understand where you fit you will need to consider what you now know about your organisation against your total industry and your direct competitors. To do this, we recommend that you make use of concepts and models such as:

- **Porter 5 Forces**[64]: A tool for understanding the balance of power in an industry, looking specifically at buyer, supplier and competitor power in relation to your own. This is especially useful when thinking about gamification as you can identify where your ideas can be easily copied, substituted or ignored.
- **SWOT analysis**[65]: Working out your organisation's internal strengths/weaknesses and external opportunities/threats will help you contextualise where you fit in the wider industry. It should also help you identify some areas where gamification might have a positive impact by either turning a threat/weakness/opportunity into a strength, or by leveraging an already existing strength further.
- **PESTLE analysis**[66]: This should get you thinking about all the external factors that are impacting your industry and organisation. It should also highlight some potential risks that might come up when implementing a gamification solution (such as if there is a lack of trust in the industry).

Don't just use these tools as they are, though; we recommend that when doing your analysis you split your research across these various aspects of your industry:

- **The market as a whole:** For our gym example, this would be looking not only at gyms worldwide, but all products/services that address the same issues that your organisation addresses. For gyms, this could be weight-loss products, home exercise and even cosmetic surgery!
- **The market in your sector:** This would be focused specifically on other organisations with a similar offering to your own. This analysis, and the analysis of the whole market, can help you think outside the box when it comes to gamification solutions, as other areas of the market may be trying and succeeding at different things your direct competitors haven't even thought of yet.

- **Your direct competitors:** These are the organisations you are directly competing with for customers, it's a you-versus-them situation. This is the most important facet of your analysis when it comes to marketing, as you need to understand how your solution will stack up against a rival offering.

Don't forget to consider gamification when doing each part of the above analysis. How do your competitors and the wider industry use gamification or game elements in their products and services? Are these tactics successful? How can you improve on them or do something different?

You should also determine the various marketing methods that are being used for marketing each product in the industry; this will be of use in the next section, as well as determining later which of these channels and services are most suited to gamification.

Competitor analysis

Now that you've done the initial work of determining your products, those of your competitors, what your strengths and weaknesses are, and what they are within the industry as a whole, it is time to use this information to evaluate how your marketing stands against your competitors. What are your competitors focusing their marketing on? Is it social media, email lists, local advertising, online advertising? Discovering the answers to some of these questions will inform you as to where the competitive spaces are and where the industry at large is focusing its time and money. The next step is to work out whether you want to focus your time and money on similar channels or untapped ones.

Take the time to have a look at some possible competitors to your business. We will use our competitor analysis to see what the common issues and goals are that they may have in relation to *The Thunder Gym*.

The methodology for this competitor analysis should use the above tools, but if possible, try to interview customers who have tried either of the products that your competitors offer. An even better method is sign-up yourself and try the services for yourself. Use their websites, read their marketing and sales materials to formalise an idea of what they offer.

Armed with the information from your competitor analysis you can start to build an idea of what sets you apart from the rest. For *The Thunder Gym*, the capabilities that you have are the classes that you offer in various physical training regimes, such as martial arts, yoga, Pilates. This is useful, as these already have an in-built element that can be used with gamification, such as individual offerings and paths, and inbuilt mastery and difficulty that allows the player to progress as they keep coming back to the gym. Each is also a collective activity and because it uses the motivators of autonomy and mastery it offers more than the basic aerobics class that simply repeats exercises to maximise burn and stamina.

With just the small amount of internal research we've carried out this far, we've discovered a few common issues and goals between your gym and a competitor and what kind of motivators the gym has to create engagement in the player. The main goal that the gym has marketing to its players is for them to improve their own health with a positive disposition to meaningful exercises. This is an important point because the end goal is the player's needs, rather than your company's revenue stream.

Case Study: *Salesforce Trailblazer LMS*[67]

As we mentioned earlier, we want to add a few case studies unrelated to fitness, to give you an interdisciplinary grasp of what we're talking about.

You've probably heard of Salesforce. It's ubiquitous in the customer relations field, and it is a really flexible platform that is used in hotel management companies, business schools, retail companies, etc. But because of its flexibility and adaptability, it has a lot of add-ons, either standard or custom-made, and this requires learning.

Salesforce, therefore, has its own learning management system called Trailblazer, where newcomers and veterans can go to learn about Salesforce. But what sets them apart from their competitors is that, just like Fitocracy[68], an online gamified personal fitness application, they've decided to focus on community and a sense of belonging.

But this isn't the only motivator. As it is an LMS, and Salesforce requires knowledge and skill to use effectively, it once again has the inherent motivators of autonomy and mastery – improving your skills through learning the platform and receiving acknowledgement from other trailblazers, which is where the motivator of esteem comes in. Anyone who is a successful member of the LMS is known as a Trailblazer. Both an achievement and a badge of recognition is given. The naming of and the connotations of belonging because of a name like Trailblazer is a powerful tool.

The essential experience and outcome of the Salesforce Trailblazer concept is that Salesforce is selling the capabilities of the individual rather than their own product. They effectively market the versatility of their platform through the empowerment and competencies of their users.

How do others see you?

We've spent time working out who you are as an organisation and where you think you fit in the broader industry. The next question, though, is do your customers agree with you?

We need to work out what your brand is and how others perceive your brand. This is important to understand because it will impact how you go about gamification.

You need to be aware that an altruistic position is more favourable. Placing the needs of your players first will win out above any other implementation. If in the implementation of your gamification solution, you place your business first, you will likely be seen as inauthentic and untrustworthy, and this will eventually lead to your players rejecting your brand. You must accept that you are there for the player; you and everyone in your company needs to remember this. If there's one thing that players of all cultures, ages, genders and ethnicities dislike and shun, it's a cut-throat, profit-seeking company.

Therefore, it's very important for you to do in-depth qualitative research to discover what the external perceptions are of your brand. This is best done by gathering feedback and impressions via surveys, questionnaires and face-to-face interviews. Through this, you can find out the general impression that customers have of you, what they like and dislike, etc. Remember to use this information to also inform iterations of future qualitative research.

A method of doing qualitative research is by analysing and evaluating current practices within the gym. What are the gym's present objectives? Do they align with what we've said before? This is a useful method as you are able to achieve multiple outcomes, determining what is currently being offered to the customer, what the perception is of the practice internally and externally, and you have the extra bonus of now knowing and understanding how this can be changed, improved and, iterated upon through the use of gamification.

When conducting external qualitative research, remember to not only have one-on-one interviews, but also group interviews, and also to try and get a mix of various demographic groups. Some good guiding questions to start off with are:

- Why did you choose *The Thunder Gym* over the others?
- What about the classes drew to you to this gym?
- How are the offerings of the gym more unique than the next competitor's?

Make sure that your vision aligns with the company leadership and the shareholder's leadership; this is done through internal qualitative research. This is necessary so that you can avoid wasting time developing a gamified experience for your players that doesn't align and won't be accepted or implemented.

As the marketing executive for *The Thunder Gym*, the easiest way of doing internal qualitative research is much the same as you would do externally; by asking questions. Discussing with heads of departments and representatives to determine the general view and feeling of what the company is about and how to move forward – using this knowledge to weave the red line within the gamified campaign so that the expectations of your players are met and align with those of the company overall.

Some initial guiding questions are:

- Would you use your own services?
- Do you enjoy the offerings at *The Thunder Gym*?
- What offerings/services would you change/improve?

An example of knowing whether our gym has the right objectives in mind is by looking at how the sign-up/renewal process works for players. If the overall feeling is that the sign-up process is the most important aspect of the gym and that it should be gamified as quickly as possible, then we know that the business objective leans more towards a revenue stream than player-focused self-improvement. If the aim is more to improve and increase renewals and stem drop-off, then we know that the business objective is more player-focused. We know this because increasing renewal and slowing drop-off are for the benefit of the gym-goer. If they are motivated to renew and stay at the gym, then they are enjoying themselves and becoming healthier. The added benefit is of course that the gym maintains its current revenue stream, but that wasn't the main objective.

Luckily, though, after all of your research, *The Thunder Gym* is indeed run by a bunch of good-natured fitness nuts. Your investigation and analysis of practices showed that the expectations and values of the leadership, the stakeholders, the customers and your own all align with each other. Everyone is indeed aiming for a healthier lifestyle that they either want to start or maintain, both internally and externally, and hopefully can be improved upon with a gamified solution.

But what if you are not lucky enough to have everything align once you have done all of your research?

If that is the case then you are really only left with two choices; one is to try to convince the errant party about your idea, or you must simply accept that gamification is not right for your company just yet. If it is the former, then continuing through this section and gathering further research and developing a prototype of what the marketing gamification solution will look like will aid you in arguing your point and hopefully convincing those that are unsure of your idea.

If it is the latter, then perhaps try a piecemeal approach, rather than creating a fully gamified solution project from scratch; use the knowledge you have gained from this book to improve engagement in various smaller areas within your company. And perhaps somewhere down the line your company will be ready for your marketing gamification project.

Case Study: *Boundless Minds*[69]

Boundless Minds is an app-developing tech start-up that isn't in Silicon Valley but rather in Venice Beach, California. And they are aiming to change how we use technology, through the use of technology. Rather than saying we're obsessed with technology and that this should be stopped, they are looking at how better to use technology like the smartphone and tablet, to help improve our lives. Not just obsess about the unread update on our Facebook page or Twitter feed.

But before they take on a client and/or offer a service to a possible client, they use a system to determine whether the client's or customer's values align with their own. They've clearly already done the self-reflective bit of the qualitative research, so they know who they are, internally, quite well. The value system that they use is to determine then how they are perceived externally and whether the perception of the possible client aligns with theirs.

The system they use is essentially asking six questions, one of which is: 'Are the actions that drive value for the publisher the same actions that drive value for the user?' The tone of this question is similar to all the others. They principally want to determine whether the publisher's values are as altruistic as their own. And if they are, then the partnership will happen and the eventual product will most likely be successfully received by the public and it will help improve the public's life.

If the values don't align, then they don't start, the partnership simply ends there. Being able to quickly and efficiently determine something so fundamental is a valuable ability and method when wanting to develop something, and it is of specific note when creating any gamified experiences. So, we urge you to learn from them, so that you are better equipped to understand your own company, your customers and the values that each may have.

Summary: Chapter 13

Before even starting with your marketing gamification solution you need to discover various aspects of your company:

- What products/services do you offer?
- What kind of people and expertise are available in your company?
- What are you able to deliver?
- What does your industry look like? Are there many or few competitors to you? What do they offer?
- How is your brand perceived internally and externally and how can you use this to your advantage?

Next steps:

- Create a document or spreadsheet and start listing down what you and your colleagues answer to the above questions.
- Either alone or with your team, run through the various frameworks to discover what products you are able to offer, what strengths/weaknesses you have, what threats are out there to your idea and what is the power of your customers in reference to your offerings.
- If needed, create a paper-prototype concept to convince your company leadership of your idea.

CHAPTER FOURTEEN

Who are your players?

Your players will be your customers and the end users in your gamified system. If you are planning to implement gamification for internal marketing, your players will instead be the employees of your business.

With *The Thunder Gym*, your players are your fitness enthused customers, and as such, we'll look at how you can identify them and create personas that fit them. These personas will help you build an effective gamified solution that aligns with your player's play style and appeals to their motivational levers.

The power of stereotypes

What is a persona? For our purposes, they are semi-factual representations of your customers. A stereotype that you can quickly think of to summon up an image of a customer type.

Personas help to build stereotypes of your typical customer groups, which you can use to better target marketing campaigns and messaging to those groups – in this case, they will help you to understand better what their motivational levers are.

The term stereotype is often associated with negative connotations, as it's linked with concepts such as racial stereotyping or biased preconceptions. But really all they are is a mental shortcut we take when thinking about a particular group of people and how they behave in certain situations and environments. With solid research and empathy, stereotypes can be a positive tool to increase understanding and effectiveness towards particular groups.

To illustrate the use of stereotyping, off the top of your head think of three different stereotypes of people that you might come across in a bar. How about: 'the girls' night out', 'the town drunk', and 'the first date'? You can probably straight away picture each of these three groups – and you can bet that the barman can spot them instantly and has their own customer service style for each.

Now let's picture three gym stereotypes. We can safely say that the first one is the 'bodybuilder', the next is the 'new year's resolution' who only lasts a month and lastly the 'Wall Street executive' wanting to tone up their belly.

These stereotypes, or personas, are an invaluable tool when used as part of a business strategy, as they can help you and your colleagues align quickly on different groups of customers, and they leave little room for misunderstandings. This speeds up internal conversations between teams, tightens up and improves any external communication and helps you make better customer-focused decisions – for example, as a thought experiment, ask yourself would 'the girls' night out' approve if the bar's owner decided to have a men only section of the bar?

Crafting customer personas

Step 1: Mine your database and trawl your analytics

Collect and compile together your customer data, so you have a single view of each customer. Hopefully, this already exists for your company, but the challenge of co-ordinating customer records, sales data, social media data and email data can be challenging even for smaller organisations.

At this stage try to pull your broad data and tie it together however you can – don't get caught up trying to deep dive into each customer's social media history, for example, wait until you've solidified your personas.

Bear in mind that you will never have the perfect combination of all your data, so simply gather enough so you are able to make a start with the following steps. Otherwise, you may end up spending too much time on analysis and be too scared to start the actual project. And we don't want that.

To get your customer data, start looking in the following areas:

- **Your CRM or customer database**: This should hold details of all of your current customers and active leads, along with any business-relevant information. This will vary from company to company – a recruitment consultant, for example, will hold very different information compared to a traditional bricks-and-mortar retailer. This is your starting point – connect any additional data you find to this system as it will help you have a single customer view, but just ensure you are within the law of where your company is based.

- **Sales Data**: This will be linked with your customer database, but in case it isn't, ensure that you have data on how your customers are spending their money and time. Don't forget to actually talk to your sales people, too. They will have a lot of personal information and anecdotes that you can use to build personas.

- **Email Marketing**: This is important to understand how your customers are engaging with you, specifically what kind of emails they read and action, but also whether they are subscribed to your newsletters or just to transactional emails like receipts and reminders.

- **Social Media**: While this data is difficult to extract, having an understanding of whether a customer follows you on social media is important to gauge their engagement levels with your brand. Even more important is the level of activity they have with your social posts and what other accounts they usually follow and interact with.

- **Email/Calendars**: If possible, try to pull data from employees' email and calendar apps – this can be important to understand just how often you meet with, or talk to, specific customers. This is unlikely to be possible for B2C businesses but will be useful for B2B.

- **Website Analytics**: While you will likely be unable to tie website activity to specific customers, it is important to understand how your customers interact with your website – what pages they look at, how long they stay, where they are, what devices they use, etc.

If you are a new business, then this step may prove to be challenging, as you have no prior data to work from. We suggest that you take certain aspects of Step 1, such as social media or trend analytics, and research what you can on market data and competitor sales data. It will initially be mostly gut instincts, but you will have a rough starting point which will allow you to return to this step and refine it as your customer base becomes clearer.

Remember, don't get too bogged down in data. It is so easy with current technology to get lost in data at this step. Prioritise and look for groups of people who act in the same way. This will make the rest of the process much easier.

You may also find it helps to have some initial groups mapped out in your head based on your own knowledge of what customers your organisation has – but be careful doing this as it is very easy to find only what you go looking for (and miss the rest).

Step 2: How do your customers act?

Now that you have your data collected, your next challenge is to look for patterns in the data and select personas you can use.

To do this you need to identify just 'how' your customers are interacting with you.

It is important that you do this 'how' step first, before the demographic 'who' step, because you will find that your customer base can be split much more effectively and into larger, more manageable groups by the 'how', rather than by the 'who'.

This 'how' will be different for every business and industry. For example, you could measure: the time and frequency of online sales, the number of helpdesk requests, what products are bought, in what order and where; online or offline, etc. For *The Thunder Gym*, you could measure how often the bodybuilding equipment is used versus the aerobic, or how often the sauna is used and for what lengths of time.

For other organisation types, some 'hows' can be split by:

- What products/services are bought? In what quantities?
- How often are they bought? At what times/on which days?
- What combination of products/services are used? Are there any that aren't used?
- Is there an order in which products/services are bought and when?
- How are they bought? Face to face, website, social media, affiliates?

We could list all the ways of how to split your 'hows', but you should intuitively know the correct way of doing this for your business. A good sense check is to ask your sales, support and management teams what kinds of customers they deal with regularly – you'll get back a list of stereotypes that should give you some hints and ideas. Just remember, though, you should be backing these stereotypes up with data, if you can't prove it, it doesn't count.

For *The Thunder Gym*, having pulled all the data you can from the gym's membership database, you've discovered that there are in fact three main groups of users: customers who only use the gym at the weekend, customers who use the gym daily and customers who only attend the gym's specialised classes. This gives you your first working segmentation, the 'how'.

Step 3: Who are your customers?

By now you should have a few groups of customers divided by *how* they use and interact with your business. The next step is to further divide these groups where 'appropriate', with subgroups based on any obvious or distinct trends in their demographics. These demographics could be your customers' age, gender, location, ethnicity, culture, job title, company, etc.

But remember the word 'appropriate'. Is there a reason you are creating a subgroup based on the customers' ethnicity or affluence? Do you think this is really the reasoning behind why they behave the way they do? Make sure you ask this question for every subgroup – you don't want to have 200 personas that don't resonate with your colleagues or make sense to the business as a whole.

If you do identify any subgroups, you should repeat Step 2 for each subgroup to understand how those subgroups use your service – there may be discrepancies. For *The Thunder Gym*, delving deeper into the daily gym members group, you see that there are two distinct subgroups: the over-60s (both genders), and the 20s–40s males. At this stage you decide to revisit Step 2 for both of these subgroups and discover that the over-60s only attend the gym after midday, while the 20s–40s males only use the gym before 8 a.m. and after 6 p.m. You are thus refining your player habits research.

Step 4: Name your personas

Once you have several groups and subgroups, name them something appropriate. Make the name instantly recognisable and descriptive of the customer type it represents – for *The Thunder Gym* this could be 'the weekend warrior', 'the golden oldie' and 'the gym bro'.

Check at this point whether your colleagues can recognise the groupings you have made. Do they align with the stereotypes your company talks about during lunch breaks? Do the names resonate with your team? If the personas are not recognisable, then do some checks and iterations and ensure that everyone is aligned with the concept of the names used. Try to avoid committee decision meetings; remember that this step is designed to increase speed and efficiency.

Once you're happy with the names, assign your customers to the groups. This won't always be a clean or easy task, as some customers will fit perfectly into a group, while others may fit into several and some may not fit into any.

A good exercise for this is to create Venn diagrams of the various customer subgroups that you have found, and to see where overlapping occurs between the various subgroups. This will give you insight into whether these either need to become one super-group due to their similarities or whether a further subdivision is more useful. You could naturally count them all as personas, or just the majority of one. As long as you're consistent. It's important to understand the ratio of persona types among your general customer population when planning your gamification solution.

The subgrouping doesn't need to be perfect; the main thing is to identify the few customers who are the perfect match for each group, so you can progress to Step 5.

Step 5: Get personal, ask why

Pick one to three 'perfect' customers for each group and subgroup and arrange interviews with them. Face-to-face is best but over the phone or through webcam is sufficient. We recommend more direct methods over emails or surveys, as either of those tend to make people lazy and they will be inclined to choose the easiest and quickest answers.

The goal of a face-to-face interview is to understand each customer's 'why' – specifically; why do they act the way they act? This will give you key insights into what drives the customer and will help you understand how to better appeal and engage with them through your marketing.

These questions will vary by industry and company, but try to discover:

- Why do they use your company? Initially and currently.
- Why don't they use your competitors? Or why do they use you and your competitor at the same time?
- How do they feel about your business? And your industry as a whole?
- What are their goals when using your company/product?
- What stops them from reaching their goals?
- Why do they use your business the way they do?

The most important thing to understand about each group is their 'why' – what is their goal, their purpose? Remember that purpose is one of the key gamification levers and understanding this will be a core concept of your gamification tower.

The opening 'why' question should provide you with a knee-jerk response from the various groups. The response should mirror your expectations for that group, based on the research you have done so far. The trick then is in the follow-up, you will need to ask 'why' again to the responses you have received. You are thus enquiring further into the reasoning of why they gave that response, what they value and why certain choices are made. This is a fundamental factor in making your marketing gamification solution a success.

If you do get conflicting answers to your 'why' questions, then keep asking more and more customers until you start recognising a consistent pattern. Do not impose an answer pattern if one doesn't appear straight away. If for some reason you really can't find any consistency, then your groupings may be incorrect – return to Step 2 and try again.

For *The Thunder Gym*, if we focus on the 'weekend warriors', after several interviews you discover that they are mostly busy professionals who work and play hard during the week, and use the weekend to rest – they use the gym to balance out their lifestyle. This is their 'why', they use *The Thunder Gym* to stay in shape and offset their hectic weekdays.

Refining the personas further

Once you're happy with your groupings and have had a successful round of interviews to understand the 'why' for each group – you may now want to go further into the social profiles of some of your customers in each grouping. Look into 10–20 different customers and try to discover any trends in how they use technology and social media, whether they have any shared interests and whether you have missed any other significant associative factors. This should add another level of understanding and complexity to your personas.

This depth and richness to each persona is important, but you need to make sure that you don't go too far. It's difficult to recommend the number of personas you will need, as it varies from business to business and from industry to industry. You will need to apply your own judgement here, based on the research you have done, and stop creating groups when adding any more adds no value, or when it becomes too overwhelming for your marketing resources.

The key to the right number of groups and personas is balance – you should stop when you start repeating key 'why' and 'how' themes, and when your research is no longer uncovering anything useful or new.

For example, you may have discovered with *The Thunder Gym*, that there were two groups that fit the 'golden oldie' persona grouping. The reasoning for the initial split was that one was using the pool area for Hydro-Pilates, while the other was using the open floor areas for dance aerobics. The preliminary rationale was that each would have different wants and needs due to their locations. But after some more research and asking the right 'why' questions, you discovered that their needs, values and choices came down to the same thing: remaining fit and mobile through their later years. Therefore, your offerings can be more based on expanding choices that fit these health needs, rather than creating superfluous choices for what were originally seen as location-based needs.

One final point to consider when creating personas is whether you want to create 'negative personas'.

Negative personas are those that are specifically categorising a type of customer that you don't want to do business with or target. These bad customers (e.g. late payers, those that complain unnecessarily, are rude to staff or other customers) have somehow found you in the past, and may share characteristics that you can group.

By creating these personas and understanding them better, you can either take steps to avoid targeting them in the future or use the insights you've gained to better communicate with them and hopefully make them better customers. Additionally, if you are struggling with the previous steps, you may use this angle as an exercise in reverse engineering to discover which customer you do wish to target. This may be useful if you are a new business, with no current customer base.

Supermarkets famously do huge amounts of work on creating and honing customer personas. They collect data through the use of loyalty schemes and online shopping records and have huge databases of customer shopping data. They use this data exactly as we've outlined above, finding patterns and creating personas around why these customers behave the way they do – they then use this data to work out what certain stores should stock, when to expect shoppers so they staff correctly and where to open more stores.

Applying the gamer spectrum

Assuming everything went well in the previous steps, you should now have a list of marketing personas that you can use throughout your own marketing plans, campaigns and communications – this knowledge and the tools used will help you to better understand and talk to your customers.

Now let's add a gamification aspect.

First, we should understand how familiar our customers are with games. Do they play games – both computer games and more traditional games and sports? Do they consider themselves 'gamers'? Have they been exposed to gamification before, in your industry or others?

This can be difficult to ascertain – we recommend asking these questions during your interviews in Step 5 when building the personas, but you may get false positives and negatives if your sample is slanted. For example, it's very easy to dismiss a group as non-gamers because your questioning was based on PlayStation/Xbox gaming which they don't do, but in reality the whole group are avid mobile-gamers who don't see this as gaming in the traditional sense.

Further enquiry into social media may help, as you should get a better understanding of whether your personas are interested in sports, follow brands like PlayStation/Xbox/Nintendo, or are active on social game apps like *Candy Crush*.

It's not the end of the world if you get this stage wrong, but it will help you to understand how much of a helping hand your customers will need when you first expose them to your gamification experience.

Second, keep in mind that people are not 'gamers' or 'non-gamers'; most exist somewhere between the two and you should try to understand where on the spectrum they fit in relation to one another. For example, with *The Thunder Gym*, neither the 'weekend warriors' or the 'golden oldies' are gamers, but the 'weekend warriors' are much more tech-savvy and interested in both sports and gaming culture – meaning they will require less hand-holding and explanation when you first launch your gamified solution.

But for the purpose of creating some oversight and a base spectrum to work from, let's examine certain generalisations and recognisable stereotypes that we have come across between gamers and non-gamers:

Gamer tendencies and behaviours

- Gamers are more critical of gamification due to their prior knowledge of games and game-like systems – this may make them more likely to abandon gamification solutions if they spot any problem areas.
- Gamers do not need as much guidance with gamified systems as they should instinctively recognise and engage with game mechanics.
- Gamers tend to be more vocal when changes or issues occur with a gamified system; they will publicly voice their displeasure and will be quick to discard gamification solutions.
- Gamers are likely to remain more loyal if they can see that a product and gamified system they use delivers value to them or their community.

Non-gamer tendencies and behaviours

- Non-gamers tend to be happier with casual gaming experiences and may find more enjoyment from your gamified system than gamers will because of this.
- Non-gamers may be less vocal in both their praise and their complaints as they only have a casual interest, but will likely be more influenced by a vocal minority or majority's opinions.
- Non-gamers will probably require regular hooks of value to keep their long-term loyalty – however, once their loyalty is achieved, they are unlikely to leave due to being in recognisable comfort zones, otherwise known as the 'comfort effect'.

What kind of players are your customers?

Finally, and importantly for your gamification implementation, we need to understand what motivational factors are likely to drive your customer personas. Each of your personas should have at least one primary motivator that you think drives them to act the way they do to reach their goals.

These motivators not only influence how they act in real life, but will also influence how they act in your game and what will motivate them to continue while playing it.

Below we've listed a number of player types from models created and expanded upon by Richard Bartle and Andrzej Marczewski[70]. These player types are descriptors of player behaviour linked to the motivational levers we outlined in Section 2. Read through each and try to assign at least one of them to your personas.

- **Achievers** – Linked with the mastery motivational lever. Achievers are looking to learn new things and improve themselves, but most importantly, they want to know that they are improving through implicit and explicit feedback mechanisms. Achievers are competitive in nature but are more focused on beating themselves and the game than on beating other players. Effective game mechanics are bosses, quests, challenges and achievements – but make sure they are difficult enough to achieve, or they become meaningless for the achiever.

- **Free Spirits** – Linked with the autonomy motivational lever. Free spirits want to create and explore in games. This could be by uncovering new secrets or even creating new content for other players – it all depends on the type of game they are playing. These player types are creative and inquisitive by nature and dislike unnecessary restrictions. Effective game mechanics for them include allowing the player the ability to customise their experiences and make decisions in how they interact with the game.

- **Socialisers** – Linked with the Belonging motivational lever. Socialisers want to interact with others and create social connections when they play games. They are more interested in the connected nature of a game or the community around it than actually playing the game itself. These are generally a game's or company's loudest fans and critics and can be vital in recruiting others through mediums like social media where they are often prevalent. Effective game mechanics include communication channels between players within the game, letting players team up and form their own groups and allowing players the ability to vote on or rank content.

- **Philanthropists** – Linked with the purpose motivational lever. Philanthropists are altruistic, wanting to give to other people and enrich their lives in some way with no expectation of reward. In games they often act as mentors to newer players and can be vital when trying to build in-game communities. Philanthropists require belonging-based game mechanics to operate well (chat features, teams, etc.), but more importantly they need a narrative – philanthropists need to feel engaged with a game, its characters and its purpose before they are willing to commit themselves to others. Make sure your game's reasoning resonates with this group's 'why' to gain traction with them.

- **Players** – Linked with the esteem motivational lever. Players will do what is needed of them to collect rewards from a system. Like achievers, they are naturally competitive, but tend to be more focused on comparing themselves against others. Players can be motivated using game mechanics such as points and leaderboards to encourage them to maximise their score against others. Players work well against each other and can form a virtuous cycle of one-upping each other, which is great for your business if their actions are beneficial to you.

- **Disruptors** – This is an interesting group as they embody the safety motivational lever. Disruptors seek change in a game (both positive and negative) and will attempt to either directly or indirectly try to change your gamified system if they can, to better suit their needs and wants. Disruptors are difficult to identify but will most likely make up the majority of any anti-personas that you have identified. The best way to engage with disruptors is directly – give them a direct outlet into your company and seek to make them feel like an agent of change. Beware, though, that if they feel that you are being inauthentic in your dealings with them, they will become very vocal critics.

You should be aware that customers will often exhibit multiple characteristics of these types and will resist being categorised into singular types or personas. As Jon Radoff has commented; your players will evolve as they go through your gamification experience, their needs will change as their experience grows[71]. It's important that you create a gamified experience that appeals to each gamer type, but you should prioritise those motivational levers that resonate the most with your customers.

Remember that this is just a theoretical – if useful – framework, and you should not be discouraged if it doesn't completely fit your situation. Instead, use common sense to identify the likely motivational levers for each customer group and go from there.

For *The Thunder Gym*, you have identified that the majority of your customers are firmly in the 'achiever' player type – this is not surprising given the nature of your business. You've also discovered that a significant proportion of some of your customer groups are also in the 'socialiser' player type. Because of this, you should strongly consider focusing your gamification solution on the mastery and belonging motivational levers and their associated game mechanics, like bosses and quests. This could potentially give you the upper hand against your competitors, who are focusing entirely on their customers' esteem.

Summary: Chapter 14

It's important to understand who your customers are if you are going to build an effective marketing gamification solution. If you get this wrong, your customers won't be engaged and the project will fail. We've laid out some actionable steps to build customer personas and how to use these personas to understand what game mechanics you should focus on.

Next steps:

- Mine your database for customer data.
- Group your customers using this data by how they act, then by who they are.
- Name your personas and check with your team that they resonate.
- Interview your customers per persona, find out why they act the way they do with you.
- Identify where each persona sits on the gamer spectrum, and what their key motivators are.
- Cross-check these assumptions with Bartle/Marczewski player types.

CHAPTER FIFTEEN

What problems are you trying to solve?

You may already have a specific problem in mind that you plan to solve with gamification, but if you do, we still recommend that you don't skip this chapter. Choosing the right or wrong problem to solve is the difference between a successful or doomed implementation of a marketing gamification solution.

In this chapter, we will show you how to map out your relevant business and marketing problems and clarify what your gamification implementation should focus on solving. Then we'll look at how you can set goals and metrics, and how to build a business case that wraps it all together.

Identify your stakeholders

List the relevant stakeholders of the business that you are likely going to impact. Hopefully, the work for this has already been done if you went through the requirements of the previous chapters.

At a minimum you should have the following:

- **The business itself** – usually the owner or relevant members of the senior management team.
- **The marketing team** – could just be you but should include the most senior relevant marketer.
- **The players you're targeting** – this could be either customers or employees as your gamification solution could feasibly impact either.

However, going forwards we will refer to this group solely as the player (stakeholder) group – these are the persona groups you identified in the previous chapter.

These are the three key stakeholder groups we will cover, as they are the most relevant when identifying goals and their associated problems/ blockers. But don't feel that you need to stop there. Think about your own business and who else should be included here; likely candidates could be: customer service teams, regulatory bodies, sales teams, internal IT, operations staff, external partners and marketing/design agencies and so on.

Before moving on, make sure that you list out in detail who the business and marketing stakeholders are; these groups should be kept informed of your progress and be involved in the planning process where appropriate.

For *The Thunder Gym*, the business stakeholder is the gym's owner and the gym's general manager. As the only marketer in the company, you are the marketing stakeholder. The gym's player stakeholders are the groups who primarily represent the personas you've decided to focus on: those who work out on weekends, the young up-and-coming professionals (male/female aged 25–40) and the older population who wish to stay fit, mobile and healthy into their later years.

What are the business goals?

Start at the top level of your business and identify what the overall goals are. This is why we recommended choosing the business owner or senior management team as the primary stakeholder for this group, as their goals should be aligned with and driving forward the business goals.

You should be able to find these goals in your business's overall strategy documents, but we suggest meeting with your business stakeholders, too, to clarify these, and more importantly, to prioritise them. Getting high-level buy-in from business stakeholders is crucial at this early stage, so take the time to engage with them now and really understand what they value – it'll make your life easier down the road.

Expect the business goals to be closely linked to financial metrics and targets. Most commercial business goals usually link somehow to revenues, costs and ultimately profits.

Meet with any other stakeholder groups that you identified at this stage, too, (outside of the business, marketing and customer stakeholder groups) and identify their goals. For now, list the goals randomly and don't try to connect or link them yet. You will probably get lots of duplicates from your other stakeholder groups, don't worry – it just means your business is aligned.

Remember, not all of these goals will be under your control or even in your area of influence. However, it is important to understand what each stakeholder values as they will judge your solution based on this.

Finally, try to make sure that any goals you list also have a metric and a target for that metric. For example, a business owner may state that their goal is to reduce the number of drop-offs from their subscription service to ultimately maintain revenues. A better goal would be to maintain a 90 per cent re-subscription from current clients each business year, with a 5 per cent increase in subscription fees across the business. For specific metrics and practices for when metrics are used, refer to Chapter 18.

You've met with *The Thunder Gym's* owner and general manager and learned from them and their business plan that they have the following goals they wish you to focus on:

- Increase revenue Year over Year (YoY) by 8 per cent.
- Increase new gym member sign-up by 15 per cent YoY.
- Increase the gym's average annual renewal rate to 80 per cent.
- Increase the gym's average class size to 20 customers per class.

You've also set up a fortnightly recurring meeting with them to discuss the gamification project, and a larger meeting to present and discuss the gamification plan once it's complete and to get their sign off. We propose that you do this as soon as possible, as it keeps all parties informed of any progress that is made or any halted processes. Ensuring constant communication and updates will alleviate anxieties and continue to keep support on your side from the various stakeholder groups.

What are your marketing goals?

Next, the marketing strategy. If you do not have one, then you are welcome to contact us, and we can help you in putting one together. Your marketing strategy should feed into the main business goals but be more focused on metrics and activities that marketing can have an impact on.

If you are working as part of a wider marketing team, then you should identify others at this stage who are likely to be involved in this project, and also seek out a senior marketing sponsor who can guide you and work with senior leadership on your behalf if necessary.

Like business stakeholders, you need to involve these people early on and set up regular communications with them to ensure they are engaged and are bought-in to your solution. Once you've gone through your business's marketing plans, meet with the marketing stakeholders that you have identified, and talk through the strategy and understand from them what their goals are, and again, how they prioritise them.

With a list of all your marketing goals, start thinking about how they connect with the wider business goals you have previously identified. Which feeds into what? How? Why? You can also list the marketing activities that feed into these goals, too, if you want, as it will help you to understand how you are currently engaging with customers and the impact your actions have on the business.

Draw this out physically, so you can see how many goals in your business link into each other – and then compare whether your marketing team's priorities actually match the business priorities. You'd be surprised how often they don't match up...

For *The Thunder Gym*, you are the only marketer, so you have to rely on your own marketing plan here. Your key activities focus on engaging customers on social media (measured by fans, likes and comments) and through weekly newsletters (measured by open and click rates); optimising the gym's website (measured by visitors and conversion rates); and advertising the gym on search engines and social media (measured by click-through rates and return on investment).

You can see that all of your activities and their goals link in some way to the business goals of increasing revenue, and somewhat to improving member sign-up and renewals. However, none of these activities is linked to increasing the gym's class sizes, so this will require your attention next if you are to increase overall revenue.

Connecting to your customers' goals

Our most important stakeholders are in the customer group. In the previous chapter you should have done a lot of work identifying your different customer groups, creating personas and working out what their key motivational levers are. If you haven't, then go back and do that now.

Before continuing, you should have a 'why' for each of your different customer groups – this is that customer group's goal(s).

Now that you have all of your stakeholder groups and their goals confirmed, your next step is to look at each of your stakeholders' goals and work out how they link together. These goals should flow from the customer to the marketer to the business owner. Try and string them together where you can – note that multiple goals can connect together multiple times.

With *The Thunder Gym*, the main goal of its customers is to lose weight and be healthy, with some customer groups also having the additional goal of learning a new skill and making new friends. If we focus on the broader customer goal of 'weight loss', though, what marketing and business goals can we connect them to? It's not easy, but you should be able to link it to the business goals of increasing revenue and renewal rates.

But are there any marketing goals that this customer 'weight loss' goal connects to? As in this example, you should try to identify where some of these goals aren't being met, or where you would like them to perform even better. These missing or underperforming goals are where you should focus your efforts when applying a gamified solution. The more focus there is on customer-level problems and goals, the better.

In *The Thunder Gym*'s case, creating a gamified marketing solution that helps its customers lose weight will directly impact the gym's business goals.

For your own business, you should choose one or two main goals that will be your game's goals. These should be focused on helping your customers achieve their own goals – but should also directly link to your marketing and/or business goals, too, if you want to get buy-in for your gamification business case.

It's worth noting that gamification is best at improving long-term goals linked with loyalty and engagement, and while it can have a positive impact on short-term goals like revenue, do be aware that most gamification solutions fail when they focus on solving only short-term problems.

The key with any gamification solution is BALANCE and AUTHENTICITY – you need to strike a balance between customer and business/marketing goals, and you need to be authentic when dealing with customers if you want to gain and earn their trust.

Summary: Chapter 15

When trying to solve your business's problems the first step you should take is to identify the various stakeholder groups within your business. Next determine what each stakeholder group's goals are. Try to link these to targets and metrics within your business, allowing you to have a visible win/loss condition for those groups.

Once you know the business goals, create and/or align your marketing strategy goals with them. Consider how they connect and how they feed into each other. Draw out a map to help you determine these connections.

Finally, connect all of these various goals with those of your customer. You are creating a balanced intersection where business and customer goals align. This intersection is then the point that determines exactly what problem you are trying to solve.

Next steps:

- Make a spreadsheet in which you list all the various stakeholder groups found internally and externally.
- Link issues, problems, objectives and goals to each of the groups in the spreadsheet. Cross-reference these to see if any are similar, these will be the starting points of your connections and alignments.
- Once the connections are made, and a map is drawn out, write down the problems/goals for your entire team to see. Return to these regularly to determine whether your marketing gamification is still on track and going in the right direction.

CHAPTER SIXTEEN

Building your ideal tower

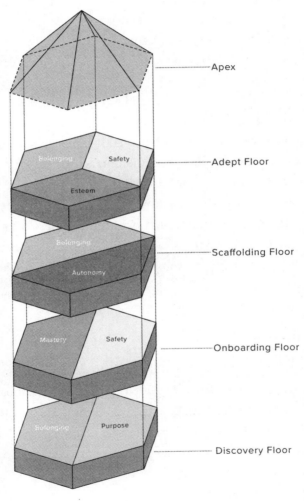

Figure 6.

By now you will have discovered and analysed what it is you wish to offer, what you can offer, what problems you are trying to solve and what kind of personas your players are. The next step is to go through and construct the various floors that will eventually become your marketing gamification solution so that you can prototype it and play-test it.

The visual and conceptual analogy that we have chosen for this gamification framework is a tower. If you wish to imagine it in terms of a game, think of Dracula's tower fortress in *Castlevania*, or for a more traditional one, any of those that appear in *The Grimm's Fairy Tales* or the tower fortresses of Sauron in J.R.R. Tolkien's *Lord of the Rings* books. The 'tower' in all of these is split into different levels or floors where the hero(es) must ascend each level, overcoming ever greater difficulties to finally overcome the ultimate challenge at the apex and save the world in the process. And much like your customers – or players – they will also ascend your gamified 'tower' to achieve their goals.

The various floors within the tower are divided into four levels. The naming conventions that we have chosen for these four floors are taken from the more common models; such as the Customer Journey Experience/Cycle and the 'Hero's Journey' from Joseph Campbell[72], to name two.

The four floors within the tower are:

1) **The Discovery floor**

   This is where your players will first become aware of, or come into contact with, your gamified solution. They are as yet not participating in it. Essentially this is the initial core marketing aspect on the journey. It is also one of the most important stages as the player will decide here whether to engage with your experience or not. As the saying goes, you only get one chance at first impressions.

2) **The Onboarding floor**

   This level is where your players engage with your gamified solution. Here you must hold their attention and ensure their retention in the experience. From a gaming perspective, you can see this as the tutorial level, where you introduce all the various aspects of your game for the first time, such as the knowledge/skills inherent to your experience and the mechanics you have employed.

3) **The Scaffolding floor**

This floor extends on the previous one, where you cement the player's interest and engagement and rationalise the choices they have made to achieve this level. In gaming terms, this is the Questing stage, where your players use the information they gained through the tutorials, and actually apply them to ever increasingly difficult challenges and tasks.

4) **The Adept floor**

This is the 'final stage' of the gamified experience. Other names for this level that you may have come across are 'The Mastery Stage' or 'The Endgame'. However, we, you and your players do not necessarily wish for your 'game' to end. Therefore, we've named it the adept floor, referring to a player who is well versed in the experience and can competently and confidently continue onwards.

We want the top floor of the tower to become like Willy Wonka's glass elevator, an almost never-ending continuation of the player's journey.

As we expand on the various floors within the tower, we will recommend a minimum of two motivational levers and mechanics from Section 2 that best fit within those specific floors. These levers and mechanics are not exclusive to those floors and can be used in any. As you become more 'adept' and experienced yourself in creating gamified towers, you may feel confident to mix and match as you see fit.

To offer an effective contextual point of view while we explore the various floors in your player's journey, we will use the player character of 'Jennifer' in *The Thunder Gym*, using her perspective to discover and analyse what each floor does, how it works and what you can do with each one. And much like the analogy of the fantasy tower, she will also have a goal at the apex of the top floor that she wishes to achieve:

staying fit and healthy while learning a new skill, such as a martial art, Kung Fu.

As a reference for the gamified solution that we will be designing here, Jennifer's persona falls somewhere between the 'gym bro' and 'weekend warrior' that we discovered in Chapter 14. As a quasi-regular of *The Thunder Gym*, she is a young professional who wishes to remain fit and healthy, by doing short, daily workouts after work, but possibly longer-term fitness classes over the weekend. So how do we get her attention and persuade her to consider the gamified fitness solution at *The Thunder Gym*?

The discovery floor

The discovery floor is where and how your players will come into contact with and learn about your gamified solution. This is true for current customers and newcomers, to both your business and the gamification experience.

Imagine it as such: the front door and ground floor to your tower are where they will discover and learn about what you are offering. Using the knowledge you have gathered in the previous chapters, you will create a strong, targeted message that will resonate and attract the player personas that you want to engage with your experience – all the while discouraging those that offer little benefit to you and your newly engaged players.

These initial impressions will be laying the groundwork for what your players will expect in the subsequent onboarding floor. These expectations should excite them and they should also be met, so don't promise anything that you cannot deliver. Be certain you know what you wish to offer, what you can offer and importantly what your players want and anticipate. If you are still unsure about the answers to these, then revisit Chapters 13, 14 and 15.

So, how will your players discover and connect with the experience?

Incorporate 'discovery' as part of your mainstream marketing

Before you begin shouting to the world about your new gamified solution, you first need to build it into your existing marketing and platforms. It should be a natural fit into your current brand and both new and existing customers should organically come across it as they interact with your organisation.

Below are just three ideas for where you can incorporate your solution into your brand:

- Point of sale displays: If you have a physical location like a storefront, consider how you will promote your gamification there. Will you have flyers by the tills, banners in the windows and stickers on the products? Similarly for your website, will you have dedicated web pages explaining your new solution? Will you have a banner on the homepage or several blogs announcing it?
- Staff training: Linked to the above, if you have staff that interact with your customers you will need to ensure they are trained and knowledgeable about your new gamification solution. Will they be briefed on when and how to talk about it? Will they know the ins and outs for when a customer has a problem?
- Affiliates: Do other organisations sell and promote your products and services? If they do, consider how they can also promote your gamification. This could be as simple as including banners on their websites, to as integrated as training their staff and offering additional incentives for sign-ups from them.

Target your current customers and prospects

You should next start leveraging your existing database of customers and leads – emailing or direct mailing your current customers with a targeted invitation. These are customers and prospects already committed to your brand in some way and are the most likely to join.

Make sure to segment the message so it appeals to their needs. There would be no point emailing a 'weekend warrior' at *The Thunder Gym* with an invitation to weekday classes.

It's important not to do this first, since if you haven't incorporated the discovery floor into your other marketing platforms as we describe above, you are likely to confuse customers who receive your messages. A good example of this would be a customer who receives an email inviting them to join your new initiative, only to go to your website and find no mention of it anywhere (this happens more often than you would think).

Actively promote your gamified solution

Now that you've announced your gamification to your own audience, you can start promoting it more widely and using it to engage with potential new customers like you would with your regular marketing efforts.

We won't go into a full list of all of this stuff (this book isn't about teaching you marketing), but we've found from our own experience that the following three tactics work especially well when promoting gamification:

- Social Media: Brands can really stand out on social media when talking about gamification – the key is to show the fun aspects of the solution and highlight how customers can use it to achieve their goals. This should include a combination of real customer stories as well as fun posts that highlight what you're trying to achieve.
- PR/Influencers: Unless it's been heavily covered before in your industry, you're likely to be trying something new with gamification and this is fresh and interesting news (probably in contrast to all the other press releases and guest blog requests you've sent out before about your company). Like with social media, focus on how this is a good thing for customers and tell real stories about how it has helped people achieve their goals.

- Remarketing: Most organisations use remarketing to push the same message again and again to their customers in the hope that they can grind them down into clicking and converting. Use it instead to promote a gamification solution to stand out from your competitors.

But these marketing tactics and tools are things you probably already know and use to market your organisation normally, so why would it be any different with gamification? What edge can gamification give?

One of gamification's main tools – that it takes directly from storytelling and video games – is the adventure hook. It is an initial quest or set of circumstances that a player identifies with and wants to explore. This is a tool used to pull a player into a game initially by connecting with their sense of purpose and belonging.

The main purpose of the discovery floor is to use both of these levers and their specific mechanics to empower the marketing tools we've listed above. With an adventure hook embedded in your marketing, you can successfully draw engaged players into your gamification solution.

So how do you build an adventure hook? Let's look at the Purpose and Belonging levers in more detail.

Motivational lever – purpose

Purpose is about creating agency and meaning in your gamified experience.

Within *The Thunder Gym*'s discovery floor you will create a discovery story that will capture the interest and imagination of players like Jennifer. This story is to display what can be expected of the experience. Purpose for our player, Jennifer, is her goal to remain fit and to achieve this by learning a new skill, Kung Fu. Jennifer's story can and will also later be used as a discovery story to entice other players like her.

Purpose is a long-term motivational lever, and thus you must use it as such.

If Jennifer is your first player, the experience itself will offer her meaning and give her the opportunity to realise her goals. Once you have her discovery story and her successes, you can use those to attract others.

These players will see that she looks in good health and has a toned physique thanks to the many hours she spends at the gym. Her success story is an effective way to promote the gamified experience. Once people discover the story of Jennifer and her health success, they will be intrigued by how she was able to achieve this.

Purpose at its core is creating meaning that exists outside of the players, that the player can intrinsically connect with, and therefore offers them a sense of agency to achieve that purpose.

Mechanics — narrative

The narrative for *The Thunder Gym* will be putting the business's core message out there to be discovered. This core message of giving players the ability to live longer, be more confident, more energetic and healthier is the red thread that runs through your fitness gamification solution. Essentially this is the focus of the adventure hook.

This message will naturally align with the players who go to the gym to achieve this. For Jennifer, the narrative for her goal is the theme of the path that best fits it on the discovery floor. Your gamified solution outlines a clear theme of quick and effective daily after-work exercise regimes, that will prepare her both physically and mentally to tackle her daily stress. But they will also strengthen her so that she can take on the larger purpose of learning a martial art like Kung Fu. Within the adventure hook, then, is the narrative theme of Ancient Shaolin Monks who practised Kung Fu and mastered it.

Weaving together this overall narrative theme, linking in with her immediate goals and her long-term goals, is what will grab her attention and engage her with the experience and lay the foundations for the next floor.

Epic purpose & discovery case study: *Beaconing*[73]

Epic purpose and meaning can sometimes be very difficult to pin down when thinking about the discovery floor. What do you put in there that will grab people's attention? Often it's the main tagline or company statement from your business. In essence the epic meaning of your gamification campaign should be in the blood of your company already.

Take for example Beaconing, an educational project that is co-funded by the Horizon 2020 Framework Programme of the European Union. As it stands on their website: '*BEACONING stands for Breaking Educational Barriers with Contextualised, Pervasive and Gameful Learning and will focus on "anytime anywhere" learning by exploiting pervasive, context-aware and gamified techniques and technologies, framed under the Problem-Based Learning approach.*'

Now this isn't the most exciting of taglines, but it does hold the right kind of information that grabs your attention. They are breaking down educational barriers using gameful learning techniques. You're instantly interested and will probably continue reading. Further on you'll learn that they engage communities, including those with disabilities, to create more inclusive and connected learning practices. We instantly have a very altruistic epic purpose that anyone in the learning sector would probably want to be a part of.

Naturally, having a more accessible tagline is desirable, but even one that has the right words and phrases in it can still help achieve the correct sense of agency and meaning in their goals and grab your attention for the grander meaning that you can or want to connect with.

Motivation lever – belonging

The belonging motivational lever targets the need that everyone, more or less, wants to be part of something larger than themselves, this is why it works well with purpose. In the case of the discovery floor, belonging offers a way to connect with others, through supportive communities and shared goals.

In the initial offering for Jennifer, it is the promise of being part of a local group of individuals who share goals similar to hers, as well as being part of a select group of people who also wish to be Kung Fu masters on the weekend. This initial narrative of belonging is what will entice the newcomers, but once these communities have formed, they can be used in the long-term to allow members to bring in other newcomers, such as allowing discounts for friend referrals.

It is worth keeping in mind then Rogers' Innovation Adoption Curve[74] (Figure 7) and where your players are on this curve. The curve is an example of how an individual's risk and change-tolerance impacts their speed to adopt new trends, but is also a demonstration of the strength of existing communities and how they can reduce risks for new members – as demonstrated by the increase in more risk-averse entrants once the risk-tolerant have established a community and safe-place.

Businesses will use different marketing tactics to attract different types of customers at each stage of the curve, with many inflating their user numbers to appear that they already have a healthy community to entice the more risk-averse majority to join their ranks.

When creating your own gamification experiences, you need to understand the power of communities and how the innovation curve

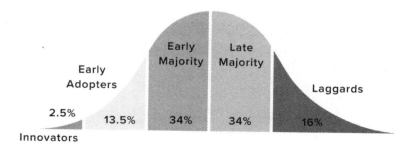

Figure 7.

should impact your marketing and onboarding efforts. Not only that, but you must also consider how you will demonstrate to users that your solution has either (a) a strong community that they want to be a part of, or (b) how your gamified solution will provide value to their existing community.

Many companies are currently using 'social proofs' in their marketing to give evidence of strong communities behind their brands and products. In the B2B industry, case studies are flaunted as much as possible to show that successful companies are using their products to become even more successful. These can be very effective if the company featured is well known or relevant to the reader, but often falls on deaf ears as B2B companies tend to blast out case studies with no relevance to the readers' needs or community.

Another example is online communities and fledgling social networks who repeatedly blast their engagement and user numbers in the hopes that they can pry away majority customers from the mainstream alternatives that they are trying to replace. These techniques can be very effective at drawing in customers, but if the claims are disingenuous, the customers will quickly turn on the company and trash the community.

These two examples are important to remember when discussing communities in marketing – they are based on RELEVANCE and TRUST. If you don't have these or if you break them, then the community will leave and go elsewhere.

The most important stage for you to consider on the curve, then, is whether there is enough of a community for the innovators and whether you can successfully recruit and engage them. The other stages will have had enough interest generated by the discovery stories of the innovators and then the early adopters to be fine.

It is therefore important to make sure that innovators like Jennifer feel connected enough with the business, until the community itself becomes self-sufficient enough to take over.

Mechanics – teams

From Jennifer's perspective, what attracts her to the gamified experience is the promotional material of people enjoying themselves, chatting and connecting with each other while doing specialist classes. The images show a fun, warm environment, and the tagline that the experience would be game-like and something that can be enjoyed with new and old friends is what pushed her to choose that specific path.

As she is an early adopter, the community has not yet had a chance to grow, but you will have created a concept of teams or houses which the various players can feel connected to. Creating teams is a very effective mechanic, which also offers you the ability to separate out your various personas into groups that will naturally connect better with each other. As long as you maintain a friendly nature between the various teams, and perhaps foment a light competitive atmosphere, then these will naturally evolve into self-sustaining communities.

Additional mechanics that are inherent with teams and communities are communication features and rankings. These mechanics are a must to ensure that communities survive. Promising and implementing features such as Facebook groups and lighthearted local rankings based on player voting will cement players' connection with each other. This also feeds into the longer-term discovery story; as players use more visual platforms, they will naturally attract newcomers to their communities, assuming the experience does indeed look like fun.

Belonging & discovery case study: *Top Hat active learning technology*[75]

The beauty of a gym is that it is by its very nature a social, face-to-face environment. It already has an essential promotable quality of belonging. But if your particular business doesn't have this clear communal aspect then perhaps a look at an online gamification business will help you come up with some ideas when thinking about belonging levers for the discovery floor.

An example of belonging and adding a competitive tint to a communal experience is with the School of Business and Economics at Wilfrid Laurier University and its use of Top Hat's learning technology. Professors and teachers use a tournament style mechanic to test students' assigned reading. The use of this mechanic boosted student morale, energy and got the more introverted individuals to also demonstrate their understandings, all in the spirit of friendly competition.

The idea of competition can be expanded upon by allowing these students to form teams to demonstrate their knowledge, much like the idea of an academic decathlon, leveraging additional mechanics such as points and leaderboards.

The onboarding floor

Now that your players, like Jennifer, have discovered your gamified fitness experience and are taking their first steps into it, you must now engage and teach them everything they need to know to be successful in it.

The discovery floor is very much reliant on what the current trends in communication and marketing are. Knowing and anticipating those will mean your discovery floor is more successful than your competitors. The onboarding floor, then, is where we get into the fundamentals of what makes your gamified solution unique, both internally and externally.

The onboarding floor is a space where you engage your players through tutorial-based interactions. We want to whet their appetite and get them motivated with what is on offer, teaching and training them in what they need to know and do to be successful in the long run. It is also a space in which you can train up players who are unfamiliar with certain aspects of your experience, such as possible technological features, or certain techniques, as would be the case with a specific exercise regime.

With Jennifer, we know from her persona profile that she is a goal-oriented player, and thus within the onboarding floor we need to make sure that she receives the correct objective-based information for the path that she has chosen within the gamified experience, so that she can get value from it straight away. That's why we use the term 'tutorial', as it needs to be a quick knowledge transference for players to receive immediate feedback and value.

One aspect to be aware of when creating tutorials within your onboarding floor, is to remember to ensure that they remain fully integrated into the overall experience. Onboarding often fails when the knowledge transference of tutorials needs to happen outside of the experience, for example if Jennifer was required to go to an external yoga specialist, unaffiliated with *The Thunder Gym*, so that she would be ready to take part in the fitness section of your gamified exercise solution. This physically and mentally removes her from the experience.

Tutorial case study: *BBVA Game*[76]

BBVA is a large Spanish bank. They gamified their website to help teach their customers that using online banking was as secure as doing it face-to-face.

The way they managed to empower and entice their customers to learn to use their online banking system was through the creation of quests and challenges, and offering them the opportunity to gain points.

These quests could be actions such as when they made an account, paid bills or carried out any transactions. They would then gain points for completing these which could then be used to buy downloadable music, film tickets or passes to football games in Spain, and so on.

The game managed to attract 100,000 new users in the space of six months.

One of the reasons for its success is that all the knowledge and skills required to complete the challenges was inherent in the experience provided. The customers did not need to go outside the experience to learn how to use it; everything was incorporated, from the start screen to the final transaction screen.

One issue that can arise with this, though, is that the points reward system could be absorbing, and customers did mention that they 'loved' how 'addictive' the game was. This can be a problem point as the pursuit of gaining tradable points for external items overshadows the tutorial experience initially intended.

Within *The Thunder Gym*, a good tutorial system is there to build and then assign players to specialist classes designed to teach them the techniques they require for your gamified experience. Jennifer could have a personal trainer assigned to her, so that she can have an even more targeted and immersive experience in the path that she chose with her Kung Fu training.

Likewise, you could simulate this with a series of onboarding emails that are sent at set time periods to new players to teach them about the different aspects of your game.

You can even use marketing automation tools to sync with your website and emails so certain emails are sent when your tools detect players reaching certain stages. An example of this would be an onboarding email going to Jennifer when she signs up for her first Kung Fu class through the website, then another if she books in for the advanced classes later on through the tutor (who puts this information into your CRM/booking system).

Advanced implementations of this type of automation can link to various scoring mechanics. Just as with marketing automation, you can associate points and scores with activities, then turn these points into levels. You then send different communications and segment your audiences based on these levels, as well as more traditional segments like location or product interests.

Getting players to learn the game

What does a tutorial look like? Using your research from Chapters 14 and 15, you will conceptualise a training model that targets the specific personas that you have identified; their goals, their interests and their values. In parallel, you will then design the model with reference to your business's goals and your marketing goals.

As we know, Jennifer is a 'gym bro' and 'weekend warrior' persona type, whose goals of remaining fit and healthy while expanding her fitness knowledge align well with the business's goal of promoting health, fitness and wellbeing in its customers. But as we know from the 'weekend warrior' persona, these are players that will generally only come in on weekends if it is worth their while to attend. And as with the 'gym bro', they seek social recognition, so they will come during the week, but only for short bursts, as their daily work lives do not allow time for longer workouts.

Therefore, for players like Jennifer, the tutorials in the onboarding floor will need to achieve certain aspects:

- Short and easily comprehensible
- Flexibility in availability and content
- Social environment
- Targeted and exclusive specialism

These bullet points are extrapolations from the persona and problem-solving chapters, based on the habits that we have observed within our players, as well as what we are able to offer. An example, then, of what the tutorial may look like within the gamified experience is to have several 'taster sessions' available for Jennifer during the week, in which she is able to try out the daily aerobic and yoga exercises, either alone or in a group. And to then have a 'starter session' with a Kung Fu master and several other newcomers on the weekend.

To add an incentive, simple mechanics like adding a visual recognition – such as a badge for attending a taster session five days in a row, and perhaps a larger certificate-like achievement for having attended a morning starter Kung Fu session – can be used. Naturally, it should be clear to Jennifer that these visual 'Points, Badges and Leaderboards' (or PBL) mechanics are the first steps in the path that she has chosen. If she continues beyond the tutorial stage she will achieve even more which would be linked with other rewards and opportunities.

Also, within the various beginner sessions, it should end with a valuable 'reward', like a quick 5–10-minute yoga exercise she can do every morning to improve flexibility, and/or a defensive Kung-Fu move. These extras should be a fun surprise that adds value to the core activity.

The way to ensure engagement in your onboarding floor is to augment your tutorials with the following motivational levers and mechanics:

- Mastery
- Belonging

Motivational lever – mastery

Mastery in the onboarding floor is about giving your players their first sense of achievement and accomplishment. When thinking about and designing your experience, have a roadmap of how you envision your players progressing through various milestones towards their (end-) goals. Consider at which points they will have accomplished certain aspects that prove that they have mastered a distinct facet.

Be sure to have these accomplishments and their rewards divided into three tiers; these tiers are associated with the following floors in respective order:

1)   Short-term accomplishments & goals – onboarding floor
2)   Medium-term accomplishments & goals – scaffolding floor
3)   Long-term accomplishments & goals – adept floor

Each floor and its inherent goal milestones allow the player a sense of progress and reflect the increase in difficulty as they progress, as the goals become further apart.

Mechanics – progress system

We already mentioned the Points, Badges and Leaderboards mechanics and rewards in relation to esteem, and these reward mechanics work well if they are tied to a progress system. They achieve meaning through gradually increasing the difficulty of each challenge that offers those rewards.

A progress system is your player's roadmap, with which they can see what the next goal is that they should be aiming for; the next challenge they need to overcome in order to master this level and move on. With Jennifer, you would have the benefit of the coloured belt progress system already inherent in Kung Fu. You would not need to devise one, but it is a useful example of a progression system that has inherent value and recognition.

As we mentioned in Section 2, rewards and PBLs are tools, not motivational levers in themselves. They are merely signifiers of an achievement. Much like the belts in Kung Fu, they signify that that individual has achieved that rank of mastery in that martial art. It also offers a visual incentive that people strive for, as the higher ranks have other coloured belts. Jennifer will most likely be motivated to keep on progressing to eventually swap her green for a brown, and her brown for a black belt. Consider how you want to visually represent your progress system.

When determining the incremental difficulty of your progress system, make sure that your players are always kept in the 'zone of proximal development' – the zone in which the player is just able to achieve their next level up, like an exam where a new student must battle an experienced student in Kung Fu to level up from a yellow belt to a green belt. However, much of the information and metrics associated with that to refine the incremental points for difficulty will only be available to you once you have play-tested and have statistics from live implementation.

For now, during the development stage, use the formula of roughly increasing the points by 20 per cent on top of the previous difficulty milestone. Effectively achieving a progression sequence like this:

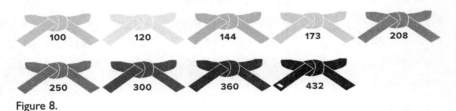

Figure 8.

Motivational lever – safety & needs

We mentioned in one of the earlier points that having flexibility and allowing your players autonomy are features that you should be aiming for. But there is a point where you cannot meet every player's preferences and demands. Now you can view this as a negative or unavoidable obstacle, but you can also view it as a positive, one that plays in with the sense of FOMO (fear of missing out), and that is using the mechanic of scarcity.

Mechanics – scarcity

Scarcity is in fact the practical implementation of FOMO. While you are creating your gamified solutions roadmap, consider your pain points. Consider where you want to offer a solution to a problem, but are blocked by an obstacle, like time or location. How can this obstacle be used to create scarcity for your solution so that players feel it is an exclusive opportunity that they should aim for and engage with?

With *The Thunder Gym*, this could take the shape of the number of available places in Jennifer's Kung Fu classes. There are only a limited number of places on the Kung Fu mastery course, and the quicker the applicant takes the opportunity to sign up, the more likely they are to be able to take part. As the class takes place at 10 a.m. on Saturdays, this may not be the ideal time for the majority of 'weekend warriors' as many of them are parents and have kids who also do sports. But as Jennifer is now emotionally invested in the idea of becoming a Kung Fu master, she will try to arrange her life in such a way that she is able to make that Saturday morning class. You have thus successfully used what was a negative obstacle to create one that appears to be an exclusive and scarce opportunity.

Security and scarcity case study: Korean shop – eSmart[77]

There is a shop in Seoul, South Korea, that has a very unique way of grabbing people's attention.

It is a local store, so its inherent comfort and safety feeling is already quite high with the local community. They know it and the quality it has on offer. This is both an advantage and a disadvantage. People may be comfortable with it, but it's not new, and is therefore stale.

The method that they came up with to get people interested in their offering was quite ingenious.

They would have limited time offers and discounts at very specific times of day, and people would need to physically come at that time of day to get the discount code and make use of it in that time period.

The method they used was that at around lunchtime, the sun would hit a particular part of the sidewalk outside their storefront that would reveal a QR discount code. The consumers would need to be there to get the code and use it by the time the sun had passed that point. The QR code would also only be valid for that day.

Many of the local business people would rush out at lunchtime to get and use this code, and it became a specific 'highlight' of their day and lunch hour to get the latest code and benefit from the offers at their local shop.

It is through their clever use of familiarity, understanding and scarcity that the Korean shop was able to increase their customer count and brand awareness through novelty.

The scaffolding floor

If the onboarding floor offered the fundamentals of your gamified experience, then the scaffolding floor is where the bulk of your experience will be found. Here you will place the methods and choices that will fortify your player's engagement.

The seeds and expectations that were planted during the onboarding floor for your players, with motivational levers like purpose, must now be further nurtured and cultivated. When we spoke about medium- to long-term goals, this is where the player will be looking to start them, and perhaps achieve some of their higher priority medium-term goals.

The scaffolding floor is where you bolster and ensure that your players sustain their engagement in your gamification solution. What you need to do on this floor with your players is to focus on:

- Keep expectations high
- Satisfy their current goal appetites
- Offer additional/different content
- Implement the unexpected (for the player)

The scaffolding floor is particularly important from a marketing perspective because it is where the player starts doing the work for you. On the discovery floor you put in a huge amount of initial effort to acquire new players, then spent even more energy on the onboarding floor teaching them how to play your game and getting them to take their first steps. It is the scaffolding floor where they let go of your hand and start running on their own (to an extent anyway, you still need to guide them somewhat).

But how do you get your players to this phase?

The method for ensuring that these points are met within this floor is to give your players their first (epic) win/reward. When designing the roadmap for your gamified experience, be sure to place a significant milestone in the short- to medium-term timescale for your players, where they take on their first big challenge and achieve their first big win. This needs to be markedly different and more epic than the minor achievements they've reached so far – for example, Jennifer's achievement for attending regular starter classes does not count as a big win.

What would count as a big win for Jennifer at *The Thunder Gym*'s gamified fitness experience is overcoming a large challenge, a 'boss fight' if you will. Within Kung Fu you will eventually need to do an exam to move to the next coloured belt, and this exam can be used to create the first 'boss fight' on her journey to improved fitness and becoming a Kung Fu master. Defeating her opponent and achieving the next coloured belt is, therefore, the big win and the epic reward respectively.

Having your players achieve one of their goals in this stage is what will emotionally invest them further into the experience. It will augment all the motivational levers that you may have been employing to this point, such as esteem, belonging, mastery or safety & needs. And for players like Jennifer, it adds additional investment in that her training and effort have paid off and she is now able to go back to her family and friends and utter the words '*I know Kung Fu.*'

But what if your players fail to achieve their first goal/victory? This can happen in reality, and we do not wish for your players to drop out of the experience because of an early failure. For this you will need to design a (hidden) safety net or fall-back for your players, so that an appropriate support structure is in place to catch them and put them 'back in the game'.

When creating the safety net make sure that the player:

- Receives immediate (constructive) feedback
- Can find or is given useful guidance
- Can retry without issue
- Is not isolated or ridiculed due to the failure

Remember that a failure should be as enjoyable, and more educational, than a win. It must be framed as a learning experience, and another step in the player's journey. Never frame it as a step back. The entire experience should be designed to restore and increase your player's confidence in themselves and in your gamified experience.

We, therefore, recommend that you use these motivational levers to augment your scaffolding floor:

- Autonomy
- Belonging

Motivational lever – autonomy

Autonomy can be a prime tenet of a scaffolding floor, and it is the most effective if it's combined with various structures designed to offer guidance to your players. As with the safety net, having a system in place that offers guidance to your players will give them a greater sense of autonomy, as they will be able to make their own informed choices about what they would like to do next. In essence you are building a literal scaffold around their experience.

The reason for using autonomy and its mechanics within the scaffold floor, therefore, is so that you can design an experience, like the 'boss fight', that allows your players the opportunity to make the decision to take ownership and responsibility for their own journey. As they've been given the initial tools and skills, they can now use them to attain their goals. When designing this floor, it is important to remember to plant the seed for this type of thinking, as it will serve when your players enter the adept floor. As they gain confidence through the gamified experience, they will hopefully start to be creative and start to think about how they can customise their own experience further. With any luck this will lead to the much-coveted state of the *evergreen mechanics*' that Yu-Kai Chou[78] speaks of.

Mechanics – decision-making & customisation

The mechanics of decision-making and customisation on this floor are about giving your players options. When designing your experience, make sure that you create frameworks that offer the player choices around:

- New situations
- New problems
- New challenges

All of these should aim to aid them in developing useful *'patterns and generalisations*' for when more complex activities or situations arise in your gamified experience[79]. You can think of this in the way of creating a guiding framework that places intermediate tasks in front of the player, designed to expand their knowledge and skill set so that they can achieve a big win on their own merit.

With Jennifer, this would be the learning she would require to achieve her first belt, the yellow belt, and also every subsequent belt. When she embarks on each new level towards her goal of the next colour the experience changes slightly, gaining in complexity, so as to denote her increase in skill.

With the increase in complexity comes the expansion of what to make decisions about and where to customise her experience. This can be done in Jennifer's case by offering more specialised classes, such as self-defence or spiritual enlightenment. This can be visually represented by a skill tree like the one in Figure 9, for example:

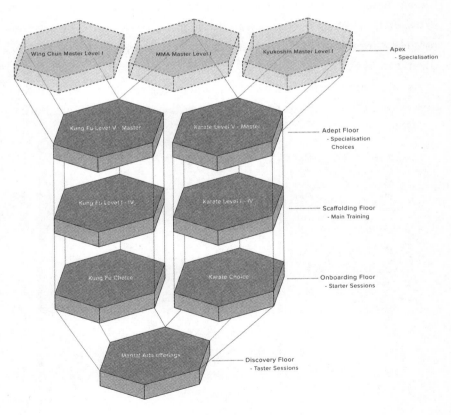

Figure 9.

Each branch is another way for Jennifer to customise her experience. And the fact that she can decide and choose these paths enforces her sense of autonomy. Think about diverging choices for your player when you design your gamified experience. Just remember not to overwhelm yourself and your players with the number of choices you can offer. They must still remain within what your research presented in Chapter 15.

Remember to keep in check the level of complexity that you will be offering your players, as it is wise to ensure that it always remains within the zone of what they are capable of. The zone between something that is too complex or too simple is an area known as *Flow* (Figure 10). Flow, as stated by Mihaly Csikszentmihalyi[80], is the proverbial sweet spot where an individual is engrossed in the activity that they are taking part in. Along the X axis is complexity and along the Y-axis is ability:

As you can see, you will always be balancing on the edges between boredom and anxiety for your players. And despite what other books

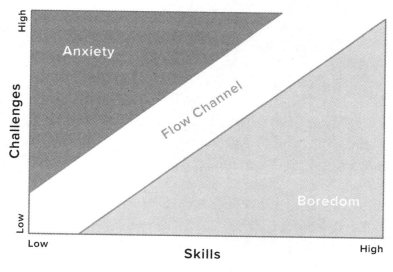

Figure 10.

or individuals may tell you, the only real way of achieving that balance is through practice, feedback, research and metrics. This state of Flow is really only achieved when the player is completely engaged and invested in the activity at hand. And it can only really be created by knowing and understanding your players.

Motivational lever – belonging

Belonging is the red thread that continues through the design of your gamified experience. It is something that we will repeat on certain floors, and it is something that you must continue to think of. As your initial players reach the scaffold floor, you will have new players coming in through your established discovery and onboarding floors. So be mindful when using belonging techniques and mechanics in your scaffold floor, to ensure that they allow for enough flexibility and interaction between current and new players.

The other aspect of belonging is that it doubles as a safety net for your players as you increase the difficulty and complexity of your experience. Make sure that your community mechanics are sturdy enough that people are able to find the help they need from their fellow players, and allow your players to take on the role of a mentor.

Mechanics – communication & assisting

This is both a game mechanic and addition to consider when designing your gamified experience. As you've planned for community formation in the previous floors, such as teams and houses, also consider the idea of allowing team leaders, team coaches and specialism mentors; they are essentially enthusiastic players of your gamified experience and wish to share their knowledge with newer players.

In the case of Jennifer at *The Thunder Gym*, this would be where the structure that you had created allowed her the opportunity to assist the

Kung Fu teacher on certain days, when teaching white belts or yellow belts; or receive assistance from more experienced players than herself. Having actual participating players helping each other bolsters a sense of community and also has the added benefit of increasing loyalty to that community.

The calm between the floors

It is worth mentioning at this point that as you design your gamified solution within your business, be aware that there will be moments of calm and silence through the players' experience. You do not need to design these for them, they will simply happen.

Player behaviour and engagement will have lulls as they go through the various floors of your experience, and it is something that you shouldn't worry too much about. You will likely see them occur as you play-test your prototype experience, and if you use the metrics outlined in Chapter 18, you will hopefully be able to determine the reason for them.

The danger of going through calm moments is that if the experience is designed poorly, the mechanics are not effective and the metrics are not implemented well, then there can often be a knee-jerk reaction. Most commonly this reaction is from those who perceive they have the most to lose; stakeholders for example.

Therefore, this is a reminder to always double check everything and make sure that everything is working as planned, but also to communicate effectively and make everyone aware that there will be points of high activity, but there will also be moments of low activity. This should prevent any panic, and prevent superiors trying to take over and push through improvised and untested designs simply to kick-start player engagement.

The adept floor

The 'crowning' floor in your gamified experience is the adept floor. Adept means that you have reached a point of mastery and/or accomplishment that is quite significant, but there is always more to achieve. And that is what you want your players to do; continue up even higher.

The games that are most effective in creating this 'endless endgame', within their own adept floors, are MMOs. A specific example of a very successful MMO is *World of Warcraft*, which continues its endgame with each new instalment of expansions to its storyline and fantasy world. It is so successful because of its engaging and ongoing story, with each instalment of its continuing story being very much a new ascension through the various floors in a gamified tower design. As the various players come together again for a new expansion in the game, they learn new aspects of the expanding world, new skills needed to explore and create new stories with each other. It's almost a whole new tower branching off of the original!

Designing a compelling adept floor experience within your gamified solution is one of the most difficult parts of the whole process, but it is also one of the most vital, as the achievements and accomplishments of players on this floor will be the stories that you use to entice more players in your discovery floor.

Let's quickly recap how each floor interacts up to this point:

- On the **discovery floor**, your new players will come into contact with what their experience could look like, as well as see the heights that established players have reached in the adept floor. You will have worked hard at this point to publicise the experience to new players.
- During the **onboarding floor**, your players start to learn the necessary skills and knowledge that will help them on their way to the adept floor. Your work at this stage is to train the players on the new experience and how they can progress further.

- With the **scaffolding floor,** your players get their first taste of victory and form relationships that will support them up on to and through the adept floor.
- The **adept floor** is thus where those engaged enough choose to immerse and master even further to open up new content and new possibilities.

Let's jump far ahead with Jennifer at *The Thunder Gym.* She has gone through her many levels to achieve her goal of becoming a first *dan* black belt Kung Fu master. For her, this is reaching the adept floor. Within your design you have allowed for new paths to open up for Jennifer – she is now able either to refine her techniques, join other masters, perhaps look into joining a Kung Fu club outside of the gym or build on her skills by helping to teach others in the gym. With the latter path you are effectively incorporating her into your design, essentially creating a self-sustaining loop for that experience.

To aid you in convincing and motivating players to firstly aim for the adept floor and secondly remain in it, for their benefit, for the community's benefit and your own benefit, we recommend that you employ these motivational levers in your design:

- Esteem
- Belonging
- Safety & Needs

Motivational lever – esteem

When designing your gamified solution, you should incorporate mechanics that strengthen aspects of esteem such as self-esteem, the internal value of the player, and esteem, the external value of the player. Self-esteem is useful as it improves the self-image and confidence of your players. If they can attribute this improvement to your experience, then they will remain loyal. Esteem, as the external value, is an aspect that has a complementary effect with belonging and safety & needs. The recognition and value of having achieved the adept floor encourages players to remain there, for the admiration of others, and to not lose out on the work they've done.

Mechanics — milestones/events

Self-esteem in the adept floor is improved through the use of particularly significant events. Remember the long-term goals that we spoke of? The ones that your players would join your gamified solution to achieve? This is where they start to realise them. If your players have multiple large long-term goals, then it makes your job pretty easy. But if they only have one, like our Kung Fu master Jennifer, then you will need to be creative in your design.

A good suggestion is to have events in place that are relevant to the personal journey of your players, and in parallel, to have events in place for the designed path of your gamified experience. Both of these event variations can also be broken down into tiers if needed. For example, Jennifer's personal long-term goal is to reach the level of black belt master. Using Kung Fu as the base example, the black belt milestone can be divided into tiers of specialisation and refinement (within Kung Fu this is known as a *dan*). Alongside this your design can incorporate parallel events such as *Martial Arts Master Level I*. Perhaps by using such an event to promote other martial arts that are on offer at *The Thunder Gym*, were Jennifer to continue and also take Karate lessons, she could, in theory, achieve *Martial Arts Master Level II*.

These are of course another example of incorporating PBLs into your system. The difference here, though, should be that these levels of mastery should convey a level of meaning that strengthens the self-worth of the player. This could take the form of you approaching your players and asking them to aid you in designing new iterations of your gamified experience. Reaching a milestone like that would have an almost infinite amount of value to a truly loyal player.

Case Study: *Beachbody*[81]

We try to use these in-sets as places to discuss businesses outside of the fitness industry. But as the adept floor is such a difficult place to quantify, we felt that perhaps if we gave an example that stayed within the fitness industry it would help you to grasp better the possibilities of what you can do.

You may have come across Beachbody before, through an infomercial, or possibly a friend who is a fitness nut. What Beachbody do better than we've seen anywhere else is their strong marketing machine, that instantly engages you in your personal need for purpose – the desire to become fit – and places it in a communal narrative of discovery. Since so many people have used it, they have a huge volume of visual testimonials.

But what they do very well is their endgame structure. They truly use the concept of the adept floor, over the master level or endgame zones. With each of their workout regimes, there is always the next step you can take. Either it's making the workouts more extreme, going down the route of a specific specialism, or 'giving' you the opportunity to 'acquire' the next set of workouts in that series. The best example of this is possibly their two flagship sets of *P90X* and *Insanity* workouts. Both have multiple versions and tiers for those that want to keep pushing themselves and stay on the journey of getting into the best physical condition they can.

And possibly one of the reasons that their model works so well is because of the freedom they give their players, the guidance they offer on time management and diet and the immediate invite into their supportive community. All of which hooks you into their brand.

Motivational lever – belonging

The belonging motivational lever on the adept floor can be seen as the glue for many of the recommended levers. It connects them with the overall community of your gamified experience, thereby conveying meaning to the player's investment that exists outside of themselves.

As with esteem, it emphasises the external value of the choice they made, with the time and emotional investment of that choice. With mastery it's a connection that is both about sharing high-level knowledge as well as engaging in friendly competition with their peers.

If your design has allowed for rigorous structures that promote communication between your players, and also between your players and yourself, or those that will help you run the gamified experience, then the expected outcome is that a self-sustaining loop of knowledge sharing has organically grown from that initial structure. The expectation is that a perpetual loop of creation-feedback-iteration-feedback-etc will exist. And the best mechanic to continue this type of growth loop is mentoring.

Mechanics — mentors

We had mentioned mentors and coaches in the scaffold floor, but this mechanic really comes into its own on the adept floor. As your players master aspects of the experience, and gain community-recognised accomplishments, they can be brought into the fold and be given the opportunity to help shape the future of the gamified experience that you initially designed.

Allowing for moments in your design where players can join as teachers, tutors, mentors and specialists in aspects of your experience's deliverables, will intrinsically tie them to the success of the longevity of your gamified solution. With *The Thunder Gym*, this could take the shape of asking Jennifer if she would like to take part in a teaching certification, seeing as she is a committed and successful black belt Kung Fu practitioner now. This offers her yet another skill pathway and connects her deeply with the gym, as it made it possible for her to get this far.

One aspect to be aware of if you use such a mechanic is to ensure that the monetary investment for your players is low enough that it does not become prohibitive for them, and also to make sure that you are not left with a financial hole in your business if you offer it as part of the gamified experience.

The benefit of incorporating your players into designing new iterations of your gamified solution is that the overall experience becomes ever more customised and new creative concepts will be added in. In essence they will be able to develop their own ideas and methods within their chosen pathways, eliciting the action of 'active learning': *'The learner (also) needs to learn how to innovate in the domain – how to produce meanings that, while recognisable to experts in the domain, are seen as somehow novel or unpredictable.'*[82]

Motivational lever – safety & needs

From the point of view of the motivation to avoid personal loss or investment loss, the safety & needs motivational lever on this floor will have a profound impact on your players. The consequences of losing out on everything they have put into the experience to get to this point will be painful and negative for them. Most players will, therefore, do anything to ensure that the time and energy they've spent to get here is and remains worthwhile to them.

This is both a positive and negative for your design. The positive is that they are fiercely loyal to you; the negative is that a great deal rides on your shoulders to continue to deliver worthwhile and meaningful new content. Though negative, in this case, doesn't mean something undesirable, but simply an aspect that will require a strong design and a good amount of work, because it is not something that you cannot deliver.

One way of making sure that you always deliver new content is by creating unpredictable or surprising rewards, like Easter eggs in a mini-game, for your hardcore players.

Mechanics – unpredictable rewards

Designing for and creating 'hidden' content in an endgame or mini-game setting that only long-term, dedicated, hardcore players can access is a way of creating a sense of scarcity, exclusivity, curiosity and ambition within those that value and enjoy your eventual gamified experience.

These hidden rewards, or Easter eggs, can be added in any way that fits in with the overall theme and design of the narrative that you have chosen for your experience, as well as aligning with what your and your player's goals are. If Jennifer received an Easter egg achievement reward for using the water fountain the 1000th time, then this would have nothing to do with her Kung Fu training, and would also be a meaningless accomplishment as you need to drink water anyway during training. If instead she receives the hidden achievement '*Sun Wukong*'[83] (named after a famous mythical figure) for having attended 1000 Kung Fu classes, then this will have a distinctly personal meaning, as well as a historical martial arts meaning.

Your players will in all likelihood start cataloguing such hidden treasures, so you will need to keep them fresh and updated regularly. But it is a fairly low-cost mechanic for keeping players engaged. The added benefit is that these types of rewards can also be used to promote your gamified solution through refer-a-friend method, or discount codes and so forth.

Case Study: *Google Maps*[84], *Apple's Siri*[85] & *Foursquare*[86]
Easter eggs are fun additions for players who take the time to explore your experience to its fullest. It is an unexpected surprise

that shows both that they haven't wasted their time and that you value their investment.

Companies such as Google, Apple and Foursquare have all incorporated Easter eggs in their products and services in some way.

For Google Maps, to promote a greater level of usage of its Street View feature, players are able to discover hidden gems such as an additional dimension to blue police boxes in the London Street View option. Clicking one of these will lead to it actually being the TARDIS from the TV series *Doctor Who*.

Another example is Apple's Siri personal assistant, who has a variety of amusing, but hidden, responses when asked certain questions. Such as the fact that saying 'Hey Siri, I see a little silhouetto of a man' will result in a long and brilliant response based on 'Bohemian Rhapsody' by Queen.

The final example is Foursquare's sign-in rewards Easter egg – such as receiving the Steve Jobs Easter egg badge if you signed into three Apple stores around the time he passed away. This is a very time-specific and exclusive (if a little morbid) Easter egg, but it does illustrate how mystery and scarcity combined can motivate players.

At the apex of the tower

Some final thoughts when designing the roadmap for your gamified tower.

Firstly, during and at the 'end' of your player's journey, be sure to insert moments where you are able to engage with your players and to receive valuable feedback from them. Ensure that each step and aspect has a metric associated with it (see Chapter 18), and be flexible in adjusting or altering them during the prototyping and play-testing phase. This feedback and metrics can be used for your internal reporting to show the success of your solution, but also to create case studies and press releases for use back at the discovery floor. The more you can show your product working, the more you can entice people with it.

Secondly, be ruthless about your design. Do not be precious about any feature or part – if it does not work within the design, and if it does not serve the player, remove it. Trying to wedge it in because it was something you always wanted to try, even though it doesn't work, will be to the detriment of your players and your business. At the end of the day your primary objective is the player's engagement and enjoyment. This is a tough one, because you will have a lot of ideas for what to include, so make sure you test each element and only keep what positively adds to the whole tower.

Thirdly, we may be talking about four floors in a tower, with the top floor being an infinite ceiling, but there is no reason why you cannot create more than four floors. If your players require more challenges then add more onboarding and scaffolding floors. If you wish to elongate the endgame experience, then add multiple adept floors. With Jennifer, we could add several scaffolding floors, each for the various belts she is able to achieve in Kung Fu, and then we could a few more in the adept floor, each representing a different *dan* in the black belt training. This gets even more complicated when you consider that you will probably have multiple towers in your gamification solution, but thinking about *The Thunder Gym*, you could create a tower for each type of fitness class that you are trying to promote, or a tower for the whole gym and its general use.

Summary: Chapter 16

When designing your gamified tower, keep with you the essential problems you are trying to solve for your players and how these align with your own business and marketing goals. As you go through each floor of the experience, regularly return to these problems and goals, using them as a litmus test to determine whether what you are developing and selling actually holds true to what your research has produced.

Next steps:

- Find a large wall and some sticky-notes and write down the problems and goals your research gave you in Chapters 13, 14 and 15.
- Determine which of your current offerings can best be altered into a roadmap and journey for your customers to engage with to achieve these goals.
- If no current offerings exist, then grab a large piece of paper and start brainstorming some that would solve your customers' problems.
- Combine the last two steps if necessary and start going through the outline for your gamified tower.

CHAPTER SEVENTEEN

Pitfalls to avoid in building your tower

Building a gamification tower, like any real tower, can be complicated and often hazardous. Most complications and hazards can be avoided as long as you have a solid plan. But there are still many hidden dangers and pitfalls that you must be aware of.

We've covered some of these pitfalls throughout the book where they were relevant, but it's worth revisiting them and adding a few extra. We will look at some of the most common pitfalls that we have seen in marketing-gamification implementation. We will outline the dangers, the warning signs and what you can do to avoid them, or if necessary, to rectify or contain the damage.

Dangers during planning

Many issues and pitfalls that appear during the execution phase can be avoided during the planning phase. The following pitfalls will occur if you don't plan your gamification tower effectively – these are the most frequent issues we see when evaluating a gamification tower set-up. And they result in players either dropping out from the game after a short time, doing the wrong things or just ignoring the game entirely.

Targeting the wrong behaviours or focusing on only one motivational lever

Humans are complicated. We are very rarely motivated by only one thing. However, one of the mistakes we see again and again in failed gamification solutions is designers forgetting this and focusing their attention on just one isolated motivational lever, like belonging or mastery.

To avoid this, revisit your customer personas and re-evaluate each persona's likely motivational levers. You will probably see that each persona favours one motivational lever more heavily than another and several personas may share the same one. There will be minor levers, too, that impact that persona's decisions – remember that these are personas, they represent the average of a group of people, they are very much a high-level view and not a perfect representation of everyone in that group so there will be individual differences.

A suggested method for mapping out the various levers for a persona is to create a type of pie chart. Identify which levers fit with that persona and then either draw it out on a piece of paper or use a program to see which lever the persona is most and least invested in. Figure 11 is a visualisation of using the six motivational levers in the tower framework for the pie chart.

Thinking of our customers at *The Thunder Gym*, you can very easily slot almost all of them into the mastery motivational group. It would be simple to just make a game that appealed to this lever using gym-based challenges and record keeping (which is what many real-life gyms actually do) – but this approach will eventually feel hollow and will not lead to the long-term engagement that you want.

Try then to explore the other levers that you have determined, such as belonging and esteem. For the 'gym bro' persona, mastery certainly is one of the most prominent levers – this persona has actively chosen not to workout at home but at a gym. Therefore, we can safely say that belonging is also a strong lever and so is esteem. If you're going to lift weights, you may as well do it with others, so that you can show off your chiselled physique. The other levers do appear as well, but each is less significant than those first three.

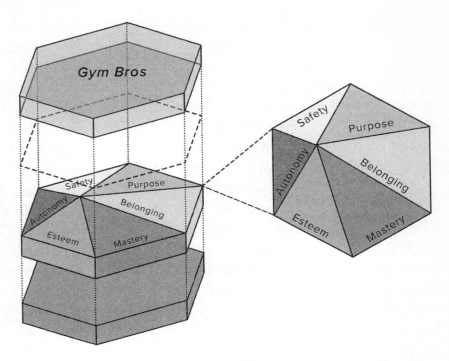

Figure 11.

Now that you know your customers are driven by mastery, belonging and esteem, you have solved the issue of only targeting one in isolation. You can now incorporate complementary game mechanics like teams, chat groups, rankings and badges, which will add extra dimensions to your gamification – widening its appeal to more of your customers and creating a much more compelling and engaging experience.

For example, perhaps for the 'weekend warriors' persona group, you could add in *Harry Potter*-style houses to divide them into competing groups. Allowing them to apply to join a house, gain acceptance and then earn achievements and reach various thresholds garners greater social interaction for players within the 'houses' themselves, as well as between the 'houses', in and outside of the gym.

Be aware to check that you are not targeting the wrong levers, though – if your players are not motivated by autonomy, for example (when using your product/service at least) then why do you have autonomy-based game mechanics? Have you thrown these in for good measure, or because you personally think that's what a good game does? Be critical and ruthless of your own choices and always double-check them. The following chapter deals with metrics, and these can be helpful in determining which are working and which aren't.

It is very easy to overcomplicate a good gamification tower, so only use what is necessary and make informed, purposeful decisions about what you choose to include and exclude. This is important, as you will likely not have an infinite budget, nor an infinite amount of time. Ensuring that the planning goes well will help with doing only what is essentially required for success, and not adding anything that doesn't add value and harms your ROI.

Forgetting the fun

Is your game fun to play? Or is it a chore?

Fun means different things to different people and in different situations, but you should get a good feel for whether your tower is fun-based by whether your customers use your gamification tower of their own free will, or whether they need to be pressured or artificially incentivised to use it.

This will come down to how you've designed your game and what it's trying to do. You can check this by running play-tests with small groups of customers to see if they engage with your game – remember, you don't need to build the perfect solution to run these tests. With *The Thunder Gym*, you could use your 'weekend warriors' group as a play-test group for a short-term, challenge-based, competitive training plan, using such things as badges and leaderboards to track their progress. Do this as a pen and paper exercise. And then run it – the only real way to determine whether they find it fun is by observing them and then talking to them after the play-test, getting their opinions and feedback.

The usual downfall of an internal gamification system is when mandatory training is made to be 'fun'. What we mean by this is when compulsory aspects of a company's systems have 'game mechanics' crowbarred into them in the hope that they will become more engaging. The makers of these systems will try to laud them, saying that people are more engaged with them. This is a false positive, as they may be more engaging over the short term, but eventually, people just take part because they HAVE to, regardless of the extra bells and whistles added to the task. In reality, these types of systems are met with trepidation by those that are required to interact with them. For systems that do not have a compulsory element, this will not be an issue, as the customer or player will simply ignore it if it has the veneer of 'faux fun'.

Building a game versus creating a gamified experience

Can a game be too much fun? Another pitfall that people fall into during this process is that they build a game, and not a gamified experience. The difference is that a game is played for the purpose of entertainment, whereas your gamified experience should have a purpose linked to your business and marketing goals – otherwise, what's the point?

The lines between the two can be extremely blurred, and constant reflection and self-checking is required. You should refer back to Section 1 if a refresher is needed. But a quick litmus test is to check whether the actions that you are motivating your players to do actually further your business goals or not.

If you built an app for *The Thunder Gym* that gave players a digital character that they could train and grow stronger over time by repeatedly clicking buttons in the app – is this a game or a gamified experience? How does training the digital character help the customer's/marketer's/business's goals? If it's purely aesthetics with no influence on their real-world goals, then it doesn't, and then it's just a regular (role-playing) game.

Instead, a gamified experience would involve a digital avatar that is only 'trained' when the customer actually visits the gym, joins a class, performs a workout, etc. The avatar is a representation of the player and gives feedback to the player on their progress: '*Wow, my digital person just got stronger – I must have got stronger!*'. This arguably motivates the player to visit the gym more – helping everyone's goals. And this statement is the key to figuring out whether you have a game or a gamified solution: are your player's goals being met through the service/product you are providing via your gamified solution, and are they in line with your own goals? A game mostly only has its own goals of achieving a win, and the player's goals are dictated by this. Within the gamified experience you have developed with the help of this book, your players should have come with their own goals, and together you are achieving what is essentially a symbiotic outcome.

Not providing feedback to players

What's the significance of a point? Why let players talk to each other? What difference do badges make? These are all forms of player feedback and are invaluable when trying to motivate players to take some sort of action or let them know if they have done something good or bad.

Not too many gamification towers fall into this pitfall because of the general obsession with points and badges in the gamification industry, but the general warning is that you should remember the point of a point: it's a feedback mechanism.

Without feedback mechanisms your players are blind to what you want them to do, or how they can progress towards their goals. Good feedback lets them understand what is helping them progress. For example, if a member of *The Thunder Gym* has the personal goal of losing weight and they are using the above-mentioned avatar app to track their progress, then when they do a cardio workout, like running 5km on a treadmill, they are awarded a progress point in their journey towards weight loss. If it also has additional information around the expected calorie burn, then their progress has added value and meaning. If the app then deducted a point when they gained 1kg of weight, and gave information on the amount of exercise they might need to do in order to return to their target weight, then they have received useful feedback. These type of feedback mechanisms help steer the player towards their goals, by providing meaningful information and a conceptual and contextual representation of their progress.

A variation on a lack of feedback is focusing just on aesthetic feedback.

In other words: Do not have meaningless points and badges for their own sake! Everything you do in gamification should link back to the player's goals somehow – if you can attach a narrative/purpose to these things, then even better. You need to think about how players are likely to measure themselves against their goals and progress and incorporate this into your feedback system.

For *The Thunder Gym*, you could give players points every time they turned up. If these points were linked to incentives you may find that they have some motivational effect, but it won't be much, and it won't be for very long. If, however, you tied these points to their weight loss or muscle/fat ratio, or mapped out their check-ins on a timeline or roadmap to their goal – you would have a very powerful long-term motivator.

Dangers during execution

The following pitfalls are likely to occur once the game is up and running with live players. You can mitigate some of these by doing pilot studies with smaller player groups – but remember that you need to keep monitoring the game once it's running to catch these pitfalls before they inflict too much damage.

Getting the Goldilocks rule of difficulty wrong

Players want to be challenged, but they also want to feel that they can overcome challenges if they try hard enough. Too often, gamification fails because designers either make their games too easy or too difficult, missing the 'just right' spot.

Too easy is usually the main culprit of bad gamification design. Many designers will be scared of challenging the player too much and creating barriers to their game, but this is actually going to have the opposite effect. If a game has no challenge, the player will not see it as a growing experience and will quickly abandon it if they feel that they are not effectively progressing towards their goals. The opposite is also true; if a game is too difficult or perceived as unfair by the player due to its difficulty, they will also abandon it, as the game is blocking them from progressing towards their goals.

In *The Thunder Gym*, challenging players to lift a 1kg weight again and again with no increase in difficulty will make many players abandon the game quickly because it is boring, not particularly challenging and provides no progress. Likewise, starting a new player off with a challenge to lift a 30kg weight may be too much and will again cause the player to abandon through frustration (or maybe pain and injury).

The key here is balance. Understand your player's likely skill level at each stage of your game and make sure that the game progressively increases in difficulty to match each player's increasing skill level.

This can only really be solved with player testing over time. Understand who your players are and how they are likely to develop their skills at your game as they progress. By monitoring where players get stuck or abandon the game you should be able to identify pain-areas where the difficulty is set wrong.

Players gaming the game

This will impact some businesses more than others and will largely be a factor of what your incentives and player goals are. Usually, this occurs when players are trying to save time or money – but is essentially when players look for ways of cheating or finding loopholes in your system for their own benefit.

This can be hard to spot, but you should be monitoring players and how they interact with your game. If certain players begin advancing much faster than the average player, you should investigate them. Best case scenario is that they have found a great new approach which you can incorporate and train others to do, worst case is that they have found a loophole which they can abuse. Thankfully, if you discover it (quickly enough), you can close it before it does too much damage.

A significant amount of the negative aspects and abuse of both games and gamification occurs when they are linked to real-world currency. You can largely eliminate this negative aspect of the 'gaming the game' phenomenon by disconnecting your gamification tower from any real-world currency. The most malicious attempts at gaming a system are unsurprisingly based on players trying to find new and faster ways of making (or saving) money for themselves – if you instead align your gamification tower with non-financial player goals, i.e. more intrinsic ones (see Section 2), then you will largely see this practice diminish and hopefully disappear.

How you decide to deal with these players is up to you, but we recommend trying to ascertain whether their actions were malicious before punishing them or claiming back what they took (if anything).

At *The Thunder Gym*, if you were to incentivise players to earn points, and let players turn those points into free sessions with a personal trainer (usually quite an expensive thing), you will see some players looking for ways to quickly and easily earn points to take advantage of this system. If, however, your tower is focused on the non-financial goals of weight loss, players are less likely to game the system as they know it will have no real extrinsic benefits for them.

Trolls and disruptors

Trolls and disruptors will often try to change your system, or actively try to annoy or bully other players. They create a very negative experience for other players and will cause them to abandon your game over time. Worse, trolls tend to attract other trolls and soon your gamification tower can become infested with them – quickly making their negative behaviour the normal environment within your experience.

Within *The Thunder Gym*, trolls could be disastrous. Imagine a collection of bad players who actively start bullying others in your online chat forums; you can imagine that not many players would stick around for long in that environment.

The best method is to empower your players to report abusive behaviour, and to monitor player behaviour in risk areas like chat forums. Have a clear and easy-to-find policy on what would require a direct intervention from your company and what form that intervention would take. For our gym troll, have a clear set of rules on behaviour, with a clear list of consequences. If one does appear, ensure that the procedure to report them is quick and easy. And naturally, make it apparent that the consequences are enforced and do happen. Not through a practice of 'naming and shaming', this we do not advocate, but rather perhaps through statistics of how many individuals were punished in the last four months for example.

The various legal issues

These should be obvious, but you would be surprised how many companies break copyright and intellectual property laws when creating their gamification towers.

More complicated, though, are the rights and privacy of your users, so make sure that you only collect the data you need to run the game for them, and do not reuse or sell on any data unless you have clear and explicit permission to do so.

Our main advice here is to make sure that you understand the various data and intellectual property laws that exist in the countries you operate in and abide by these at all times. If you are not sure what they are or how broad the purview of these laws is, then please do consult a lawyer, solicitor or a recognised specialist within the rule of law of the business, sector and country you are working in. Finally, make sure that any decision you make regarding your gamification tower goes through the ethical lens of 'is this right for the customer?' and 'will this damage our trust and relationship with the players?'. Answering these questions at the start should hopefully give you a guiding line of what correct procedure and what advice you may need.

Obsessive behaviour

Finally, you should be aware of how your game could cause obsessive behaviours in your customers. We know what you're probably thinking at this stage, but trust us, while having an obsessive platform will improve your engagement and help your goals in the short term, it will ultimately lead to player burnout and negative PR.

At *The Thunder Gym*, creating a gamified platform that causes obsessive levels of gym attendance may help your players reach their goals of becoming healthier, but it will have unforeseen impacts on other areas of their lives, such as players becoming too obsessed with attending the gym and neglecting other important social and monetary aspects of their life. It may even lead to injury. Eventually, this will have a long-term impact on their mental and/or physical health, which will then impact their ability to keep up their extreme habit and they will ultimately burnout.

We'll remind you of a phrase we've used several times throughout the book – look after your players first.

Summary: Chapter 17

Rigorous and well-thought-out planning from the very beginning of your gamified experience is important to avoid any of the major pitfalls during design and implementation. Working through the research you do on your own business and the target personas will give you an idea and a working concept of what is needed to attract and engage your customers. Selecting what is necessary, then, in terms of motivational levers and mechanics will help you deliver your desired experience. But remain vigilant and aware that even the best-designed experiences can run into problems, so be ready, and don't worry, testing and iteration is all part of it.

Next steps:

- Have your spreadsheet at hand of the research you did on your business and your persona groups – do the motivational levers and mechanics that you've selected align with these?
- Create a pen and paper prototype to test with your colleagues and then with a focus group of strangers or customers.
- Review with your team any issues you have spotted and be ruthless in what is needed to change and improve the overall deliverable.

CHAPTER EIGHTEEN

Measuring your gamification tower

This final chapter is dedicated to measuring your gamification efforts. Too often this subject is ignored or glossed over when it comes to gamification. We believe this is one of the reasons why gamification has historically struggled to reach mainstream implementation in businesses and their marketing campaigns.

Marketing has arguably gone through a similar journey – starting as a fluffy unmeasured 'art form' before turning into a hard business science that relies on automation and data analysis (depending on where you work of course). Marketing seems to have now found a happy medium, though, between creativity and data.

This balance is where we want gamification to be in businesses, but this won't be realised unless we can reliably measure and report on gamification's impact in the same way that we are expected to report on marketing campaigns.

The big hurdle to measuring gamification – attribution

ROI (return on investment) is the main performance measurement that every business wants to use when implementing a project, such as one that uses gamification. ROI, for those unfamiliar, is the amount of time and money that you put into something, compared to the benefits you receive in return over that time.

Business stakeholders will often use revenues and ROI as the key benefits to measure success, but players will substitute this for their own goals and objectives which will almost certainly not be linked to your revenue.

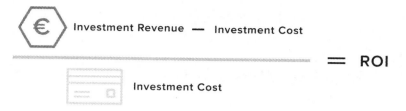

Figure 12.

So how do you balance the often very different needs of the business and the customer?

This balance between stakeholders and players is crucial – you have to understand that short-term goals are not effective in gamification, but the longer-term goals of retention and customer engagement are directly linked to customers achieving their own personal ROI. What this means is that players achieving their own personal ROI in the short term will lead to you achieving a high business ROI in the long term.

But how do you measure a gamification project's ROI?

Unless you have actions in your gamification solution that directly link to business and marketing objectives (like signing up for a new service trial, referring a friend or completing a marketing survey) it will be difficult to directly attribute and measure the gamification solution's impact on these objectives.

If we think about *The Thunder Gym*, we could measure a gamification solution's financial ROI if it drove players to actively sign up for more classes, but how would we know if it impacted gym goers' renewal rates? There are countless mitigating factors that we can't control or measure, so how can we track gamification's impact?

The 'trick' here is to segment your customers' data.

Divide your customers up between those who are actively engaged with your gamification solution and those who are not. Actively engaged is very important, so make sure to mark when a customer becomes engaged, i.e. starts to use the gamification solution. And when they stop being engaged, i.e. stop actively using/engaging with whatever solution and game elements you have launched.

With that segmentation done, you will be able to measure ROI via the following methods:

1) **'Before versus After' implementation**: A rough estimate is to look at the difference in metric numbers after you have launched your gamification solution and compare them to the equivalent metric numbers in the previous month/year/trailing 12 months. Any difference in metrics and their rate of growth or decline can be attributed to the changes your solution has made. However, note that this is a very messy attribution as it is impacted by any other activities you are doing simultaneously, as well as general market factors which you may or may not be aware of (competitor pricing, inflation, new market entrant, etc). This 'before versus after' analysis obviously requires you to have accurate benchmark data.

2) **'Before versus After' customer behaviour**: A slightly more accurate approach is to compare a customer's behaviour before and after they become an active user of your gamification solution. This is a good way to measure differences in the engagement of your customers and how you have impacted this with your solution, but your ROI calculation will still be impacted by the same external factors as above, and this analysis can only really be used on current customers, not new ones.

3) **Control groups**: The most accurate method we can recommend to measure ROI is to launch your gamification solution as a test – with a test group and a control group. Pick a random sample of your customers (try to get an equal amount from each of your customer persona groups) and assign them to either the test group or the control group. Let the control group carry on as normal, but launch

the gamification solution with the test group. Let the test run for as long as necessary to achieve a level completion with the chosen goals. Compare the two groups against one another to ascertain the effectiveness of your solution on customer behaviour. If you want to be more thorough, run several tests over several months using different control and test groups.

These three methods are what we recommend in order of complexity and accuracy for you to measure your metrics, but what metrics should you measure? ROI makes most people immediately think of revenue, but is this the main goal of your business and marketing team?

Beyond ROI: The HEART framework

A useful tool that has been used within the gamification and UX industry is Google Venture's HEART framework[87]. For those unfamiliar it measures five aspects of a project, so let's break down each aspect and how it fits into our framework and gamification project:

- **Happiness:** This is a qualitative measurement, of how satisfied your players are with your gamified project. This can be determined through surveys, or 'like' buttons for example. It is a vanity metric and it is difficult to determine whether the player is satisfied because the project is a success or simply because it is easy to use. But it gives a broad sense of player disposition towards the experience.
- **Engagement:** This is the most straightforward measurement, as it directly looks at how active your players are, through hits or uses per day, week, etc. Though remain aware that with any project there will be high activity periods, and lulls periodically.
- **Adoption:** Adoption is for the 'new' player and directly references the usefulness and effectiveness of your marketing and social network presence. How many 'new adopters' has your gamified project brought in?

- **Retention:** Essentially the flip side of the coin for the Adoption metric, in that this looks at how many active players remain over time, and what their renewal rate is.
- **Task Success:** This one is an internal measurement and should be used as such. It measures the overall effectiveness of the various aspects of your gamified project – such as how long did a sign-up take and how can it be made more efficient, or how long did it take a player to reach a certain milestone and was this the most effective route for them.

Each of these five aspects is then divided along an X-axis. Now the important characteristic of the framework is knowing the X-axis divisions, as these will be what you can take on board and act upon to alter and improve your gamified project:

- **Goals:** We recommend revisiting the work you completed earlier in the book, looking at the three types of goals that you are trying to reach: player goals, marketing goals and business goals. This will help you choose the right metrics to measure your progress and effectiveness.
- **Signals:** Signals break down the goals into their inherent parts of how they would be seen as successful or failing. An example is a goal of increasing player engagement, the signal is a 30 per cent increase in a desired action of a player, like their click-through rate.
- **Metrics:** Here we come to the actual hard cold data. Using your goals and signals, you should be able to determine which measurement tool is best suited. In the case of the above example, it would most likely be something like Google Analytics, or another popular tool, to measure and gain data on engagement and CTR (click-through rate). We had also mentioned surveys, others are SEO (search engine optimisation) metrics, satisfaction ratings, net promoter scores and so on.

Be aware, though, that not every point may be relevant to your project, but it is always worthwhile to consider each one.

	Goals	Signals	Metrics
Happiness			
Engagement			
Adoption			
Retention			
Task success			

Figure 13.

Review the information you considered when doing the work from the previous chapters to see how a framework like this can be used for your project. There are of course other frameworks out there, but we have found that this one is best suited to gamification. It is also worth mentioning that this framework links to the Google Design Sprint[88], which may be of interest if you wish to expand upon Chapter 17's 'next steps' prototype exercise.

Be aware, though, that anything offline, in other words in the real world, is incredibly difficult to measure; while anything online is more easily measurable and should, therefore, be linked through your choice of the various e-commerce or CRM systems available.

Is your game good for your business?

Now that you have a base understanding of measuring ROI and what kind of tools are available to you, the next question is whether your game or gamified experience is good for your business?

To effectively answer this question, we will break down the various measurable aspects from the point of view of *The Thunder Gym*.

First list out all of your business, marketing and customer goals that you identified in Chapter 13, and if you used the HEART framework from the previous section.

Using another framework to augment your measurements, determine or re-check whether they are SMART goals? Does each goal indeed have a clear metric that can be used to measure it? Do you have a reliable method to measure each goal?

If you answered 'no' to any of these questions, try to rectify it before continuing or come up with a valid reason as to why the answer has to be 'no'.

Business goals

Business goals will be how your senior stakeholders review and judge your gamification solution. These are the people who will care how you are measuring the ROI and whether gamification is a good addition to the business, or an extra expense with no real proof of performance.

Your business goals will likely be the most removed from your game's activities, but you should check whether you can directly attribute any particular game element or player activity to a business goal at this stage. Make sure to measure this specifically and report on any difference the gamification solution makes. Otherwise, revert back to our ROI measurement methods at the start.

To communicate progress, set up monthly reports on all business goals and their metrics. We recommend measuring month over month, year over year and trailing 12 months (TTM) versus previous TTMs to get a clear picture of gamification's impact on each metric. Also, remember to set targets for each relevant metric that your gamification solution should impact, this should be relevant to the size and scope of your solution.

We also suggest quarterly review meetings with this stakeholder group to look at your gamification solution's impact on the business, discuss any proposed changes to the solution and to review how the solution is meeting its targets or not – and any actions that should be taken to address this.

Marketing goals

This will follow the same procedure as business goals but with different stakeholders and metrics. Your marketing goals are likely to have a direct connection with your gamification solution's outputs, however, so look to find direct causation between the game elements and your marketing metrics.

We advise running metric reports on a weekly and monthly basis for marketing goals, this should help you spot trends between customer usage and your marketing metrics – and allow you to test and tweak your game to maximise those outputs.

You should meet at least monthly with marketing stakeholders to discuss the gamification solution, plan upcoming tests and changes and review progress against marketing and business goals in advance of the quarterly business meetings. This helps you to anticipate problems and shortfalls before key stakeholder meetings and should hopefully give you time to solve problems.

Customer goals

Customer goals may be difficult to measure based on what your company's products and services are. For *The Thunder Gym*, if we focus on the customer goal to lose weight, we can only measure and report on this if the customer is actively logging their weight changes with the company. You can gear your gamification solution to help you with this by encouraging your customers to log goal-relevant data with you as a means of recording their own progress.

This is important, as if you can directly show players how playing the game is helping them to achieve their goals, then not only will they double down on their engagement with your solution, but you can also now use this data (where appropriate) in your marketing material to get more players to sign up.

If establishing direct ROI is difficult or impossible for your solution, showing player progress metrics towards their personal goals is a good substitute for a forward thinking business. This data is a clear indicator of the value of your gamification solution to your customers, and therefore to your company.

We recommend that you run focus groups with real customers (remember to get a good sample from each of your customer personas) annually, as well as whenever you launch big changes to how your game works. These focus groups should be used to sense check how customers feel about your game, and whether they believe it is helping them achieve their goals. Use the session to understand key pain points within your business and game, but also to generate ideas for how you could develop your gamification solution further.

Is your game good for players?

So you've now got a list of business, marketing and customer goals and their associated metrics which you are measuring your gamification solution by. You should also have set up some regular reporting, and meetings to discuss progress with all of your key stakeholders.

But you're not done yet. Now that you've designed and built your gamified experience, you need to maintain it. But games are very complicated machines with lots of moving parts once they are running and have live players in them – you could, as it were, lose a finger if you're not careful…

We recommend setting up reporting for a few key metrics that will help you understand the health of your game, and diagnose any problems as soon as they start to manifest. These metrics are:

- **Total players**: The total number of players of your game and their growth/decline over time is an important overall metric to show just how many customers your solution is impacting. You can supplement this with the number of players as a percentage of the total number of customers your business has; this is a very good ratio to show to business stakeholders.

- **Active player ratio**: Following on from total players, you should be able to measure the number of players who are actively engaging with your solution on a daily/weekly/monthly basis over a set time period. This ratio helps you to understand whether the game is effective at engaging with customers or if it is just a novelty. It should also help you see trends in usage over time which is a good indicator for whether the game needs a refresh (or relaunch).

- **Usage**: The amount players are using the different elements of your gamified experience. This will obviously vary between solutions, but could include things like: forum posts, how often they log in to the app, how often they complete an action, how often they succeed or fail, etc. This data helps you to understand which elements of the game are most used and by which player types; it is a good indicator of whether players know or value the different elements of your game, and it can show you where you need to develop the game further based on player activity and preferences.

- **Player progress**: Where do players get stuck, or worse, where do they abandon your game? Depending on your solution, you should be able to see where your players are pooling (either on 'bosses', levels, challenges, etc). This is a good indicator that this stage of your game is either too difficult, too boring or lacking clear directions for players. It's useful to monitor this metric over time to see how new players react to changes that you make, or how different player types react to the same content and game mechanics.

- **The number of complaints and bug reports**: This is a very obvious indicator of player unhappiness; you should know how many customer complaints and bug reports come in that are relevant to an area your gamification solution provides or enhances. Monitor how this changes over time and what player types are submitting these reports – it will help you address the root causes of the problems better.

- **Monitoring for abuse (of the game, of other players)**: This is not directly a metric in reference to ROI, but it is still valuable to measure. The issue with it is that it can be hard to spot, but it is recommended that you monitor your players and how they interact with your gamified experience. For example if you notice that a player is progressing faster than the average player, you should investigate this. Best case scenario is that you can incorporate a new approach that improves your experience; worst case is that you now know where the problem lies and you are able to close it down before it causes more issues. With player-on-player abuse, as recommended in Chapter 17, give players the ability to report one another so you can then monitor and act on these reports as they arise.

Don't fall into the trap of believing that once you have launched your gamification solution that you are done with it. This happens to too many designers who then forget to monitor metrics like the ones we have outlined. To stay on top of your game, we advise daily and weekly reports on these operational metrics – these should be your red flags that can be actioned quickly or that need a quick action to stop them escalating.

However, this is a very reactive approach to managing your solution.

You should be able to spot weaknesses or areas for improvement using the metrics we've outlined, and you should use these to come up with new methods of engaging with your players. For example, you could try tweaking the difficulty of challenges to improve drop-off rates, introduce brand new game elements or renovate your game's aesthetic design and functionality to improve its appeal.

Remember to measure your metrics against historical comparisons to gauge how much they change over time and to pick up trends. This is important if you are testing new game elements and functionality to see whether it is having the desired impact.

These metrics will help you make informed decisions about what to change about your game over time, and potentially whether your game needs a complete redesign. Be aware that this is an iterative process where you improve over time based on your learnings; even if your solution is not a success to begin with, careful and considered changes can quickly turn it around.

Summary: Chapter 18

Metrics are one of the most important elements of any marketing-gamification solution. You need to be able to measure the effectiveness or lack thereof of your delivered experience. Use the ROI formula to determine the initial outcome of your implementation. Augment this measurement with the HEART framework so that you have more directed and measurable points within your solution and cross-reference these with the various business, marketing and customer goals that have been with you since the start of this section.

The final bit of advice is not to be married to the concept – it will change, and if you are measuring effectively, then it will change for the better. Anything that iterates, improves and evolves will be more suited to the situation and expectations of its customers.

Next steps:

- Draw up your own HEART framework outline and fill it with the various goals, signals and metrics that connect with each other.
- Run through your SMART goals again, double-check the work you did earlier in Chapter 13 and incorporate these into your overall measurement structure.
- Test, iterate, retest, reiterate and so on, until you run out of time and money and need to implement it – the more you test and check the better!

Conclusion

Here we are.

Not at the 'end', as there are no real endings, but at a fork in the road. We will go in one direction, and you will go in another, using the knowledge and insights from this book.

But before we part ways, we have a few closing thoughts for you to consider as you continue your journey.

As you've now finished the book, we invite you to return to some of your early assumptions and the steps you took at the end of each chapter. Reflect on what you wrote down and what you've learned as you progressed. Update and/or change those assumptions and ideas, as you've probably expanded them since the first few chapters.

This is especially true now you've gone through Section 3, as you will have gathered new data and collated existing data about your customers, your business and your goals. Incorporate these into your initial hypotheses and build upon these with the knowledge you now have.

Gather your team and reflect with them as well, offering each other feedback and suggestions on the process that you have gone through. If you have completely built a marketing-gamification solution while working through the book then review what you have come across. Use the adoption curve discussed in Chapter 16 and evaluate what attracts the early adopters on your solution. Ignore the rest of the curve at this point; focus on what draws in those customers and refine it.

Use the data you collected from this process to yet again test some of your original expectations. Do they align with what you predicted? What is different and what is the same? What was different about the outcome versus the prediction? Keep asking more questions, involve your team and then use the answers to adjust, refine and perhaps alter the various floors in your tower to better suit these new learnings.

Game over? Or continuing the experience

One common question we get at this stage is: how does the experience continue?

During the initial creation and planning phases of your solution, consider and design a summarised roadmap for what the experience could look like, post-launch. Only make a summary or treatment of this roadmap, as you haven't launched yet. During the planning and execution phases, return to this summary, and update it.

Once you have a successful launch, revisit it again and see what still holds true, what has changed and can be expanded upon and what is new that needs to be added.

You should have a rough idea based on your marketing goals and the narrative you have chosen as to how you want the solution to continue beyond the primary launch. If you are struggling with this, then return to your customers and gather more feedback and data from them. Don't be afraid to determine what unmet needs they have and which expectations haven't been fulfilled. Knowing these will give you the information to continue and retain loyal and happy customers.

Whatever form the continuing experience takes, remember that it always needs to incorporate certain core aspects:

- Delivering on promises and customer expectations
- Adding new content and new expectations for that content

Be aware that your audience may change over time, though. It may even change during your planning phase, so remain vigilant, always checking, testing and updating your persona profiles. Many an unmet need and expectation occurs because what was delivered was not what the new audience wanted in the first place.

Additionally, keeping up to date with your audience means you are innovating for them, thereby continuing to keep yourself relevant – getting closer to the dream of the self-sustaining loop of a good gamification experience.

Expansion or termination

Another question when considering continuing the experience is whether an expansion is required or what its termination point is?

Reflect on the metrics you've gathered before and during the delivered gamification experience. Do the numbers show an increase in interest? Does the increase in interest, customer adoption and subsequent revenue allow for expansion? And with that do you have enough proposed and conceived content to expand? Does the budget cover this?

Checking your ROI on revenue and profit will be the most important aspect of whether you can expand or whether the experience has a termination point. Equally, you need to consider whether you and your team learned enough from planning and launching the experience to warrant an expansion. Was it comfortable enough building it that you wish to continue? Or perhaps it is a 'single-serving' experience that is simply self-contained for a certain period of time.

Terminating an experience, therefore, comes in two sizes. One is that there is a clear start date and a clear end date. The support and content only last for so long, and that's it. Much like a five-course meal or a TV series, at some point, the resources and narrative are exhausted.

The second form is that for some reason there is a lack of continued support and/or interest for your experience – either from the organisation, your team or the customers. This is an unfortunate reality, but a reality nonetheless. People's attention will wane and they will wander off to find newer (better) things on offer.

At that point you only have two options: try to innovate (if you haven't been doing that already) and hope to retain your customers. Or the more likely outcome, you simply discontinue the experience. One piece of advice you can take away from the gaming industry is that you shouldn't let older offerings linger. Have a clear end date, even if that end date is years away, but have an end date. Having that means you can use your new learnings and innovations in a new version of the experience – a bigger, better, flashier Version 2.0 of your marketing-gamification solution.

'Final' advice

Our final advice to you before you put down this book is just a few simple points to keep in mind when working through your marketing-gamification solution.

Avoid over-complexity and over-documenting

We have given you a lot of tips, methods, processes and more throughout the book. And much of that will result in a lot of paperwork. But be careful not to overdo it. Try to keep everything as simple as possible; you need to be able to maintain an easy and comfortable overview of everything and not be required to read several volumes of operational documentation to be able to understand and deliver your solution.

Always be testing

Burn this statement into your mind. At whatever stage you are, test. Test assumptions, test processes, test deliverables. We highly recommend that you create paper prototypes as often as you can. The earlier you start with testing your marketing-gamification solution, the more likely it is to succeed when launched. Too many people leave it until they have a completed version before testing, often meaning they have too little time, no budget or worst of all, need to redo large chunks because of a late test.

Perfection is the enemy of finished

In contrast to the last statement, you should avoid over-testing. Do not get into an endless loop of testing and improving, testing and improving, without ever launching the end product. You won't have the time or budget for it, and at some point, you literally need to tell yourself: *It's as finished as it's ever going to be.* You need to launch it, so pick and stick to a deadline and make it as close to perfect as you can.

Remain calm

For your own health, sanity and that of your team; remain calm. Check assumptions regularly, communicate consistently and try not to stress. Stressing, becoming anxious and all these negative emotions will lead to mistakes. Remember, failure is part of the learning process, it's even part of the solution for your customers, so embrace it.

It's for the players

Lastly, focus on solving the player's problems. The majority of failed gamification solutions have failed because they didn't remember this. If you focus solely on your own gains, the players won't do what you want (or even participate in the first place). Your marketing-gamification solution is there to primarily solve the player's issues and problems, with your goals as secondary. This leads to happy players, who are happy customers, which leads to a happy business.

Addendum

We want to thank you for reading our book. It has been a few years in the making, and we sincerely hope it has helped you in some way in building and/or providing a better understanding of marketing-gamification solutions. If it has indeed helped you then please do share the knowledge with others, so that we all can have more meaningful and better marketing-gamification experiences.

Endnotes – References

1 Chou, Y. K. Octalysis Framework. Available: https://yukaichou.com/ gamification-examples/octalysis-complete-gamification-framework. Last accessed 20th April 2019.

2 Chou, Y. K. (2015) *Actionable Gamification: Beyond Points, Badges, and Leaderboards.* Octalysis Media.

3 Chou, Y. K. What is Gamification. Available: https://yukaichou.com/ gamification-examples/what-is-gamification. Last accessed 20th April 2019.

4 Burke, B. (2014) *Gamify: How Gamification Motivates People to Do Extraordinary Things.* Routledge.

5 Burke, B. (2014) Gartner Redefines Gamification. Available: https://blogs. gartner.com/brian_burke/2014/04/04/gartner-redefines-gamification. Last accessed 20th April 2019.

6 Werbach, K. (2012) *For the Win: How Game Thinking Can Revolutionize Your Business.* Wharton Digital Press.

7 Werbach, K. (2012) *For the Win: How Game Thinking Can Revolutionize Your Business.* Wharton Digital Press, pp. 26.

8 Suits, B. (2005) *The Grasshopper: Games, Life and Utopia.* Broadview Press.

9 Rollings, A. and Morris, D. (2003) *Game Architecture and Design: A New Edition.* (1st ed.) New Riders, pp. 38.

10 Gabrielle, V. (2018) The Dark Side of Gamifying Work. Available: https:// www.fastcompany.com/90260703/the-dark-side-of-gamifying-work. Last accessed 20th April 2019.

11 Fumagall, S. (2015) 01/12/2015 in Gamification by Shane Fumagall LinkedIn: Using Gamification to Make People Come Back Every Time. Available: https://gamificationplus.uk/linkedin-using-gamification. Last accessed 20th April 2019.

12 Wolfe, D. B2B Gamification: How Autodesk Used Game Mechanics for In-trial Marketing. Available: https://www.marketingsherpa.com/video/ b2b-gamification-in-trial. Last accessed 20th April 2019.

13 Florentine, S. (2014) How Gamification Makes Customer Service Fun. Available: https://www.cio.com/article/2378252/consumer-technology/how-gamification-makes-customer-service-fun.html. Last accessed 20th April 2019.

14 (2011) News Badges: The 'Gamification' of Google. Available: https://www.insegment.com/blog/news-badges-the-gamification-of-google/. Last accessed 20th April 2019.

15 Lopez, J. (2011) Marriott Makes Facebook Game for Recruitment. Available: http://www.gamification.co/2011/06/24/marriott-makes-facebook-game-for-recruitment. Last accessed 20th April 2019.

16 (2015) Gamification Case Sudy: M&M's Eye Spy Pretzel. Available: http://www.digitaltrainingacademy.com/casestudies/2015/06/gamification_case_study_mms_eye_spy_pretzel.php. Last accessed 20th April 2019.

17 Huizinga, J. (1950) *Homo Ludens: A Study of the Play-Element in Culture.* NY, Roy Publishers, pp. 1.

18 (2019) History of Games. Available: https://en.wikipedia.org/wiki/History_of_games. Last accessed 20th April 2019.

19 Gee, J. P. (2007) *What Video Games Have to Teach Us About Learning and Literacy.* Palgrave-Macmillan, pp. 2.

20 (2019) Digital Video Game Trends and Stats for 2019. Available: https://filmora.wondershare.com/infographic/video-game-trends-and-stats.html. Last accessed 20th April 2019.

21 (Apr. 13, 2018) Mobile Revenues Account for More Than 50% of the Global Games Market as It Reaches $137.9 Billion in 2018. Available: https://newzoo.com/insights/articles/global-games-market-reaches-137-9-billion-in-2018-mobile-games-take-half/. Last accessed 20th April 2019.

22 (Feb. 12, 2019) Newzoo Estimates esports Revenue Will Eclipse $1 Billion this Year. Available: http://www.espn.com/esports/story/_/id/25975947/newzoo-estimates-esports-revenue-eclipse-1-billion-year. Last accessed 20th April 2019.

23 (Feb. 12, 2019) Newzoo: Global esports Market Will Exceed $1 Billion in 2019. Available: https://www.gamesindustry.biz/articles/2019-02-12-newzoo-global-esports-market-will-exceed-USD1-billion-in-2019. Last accessed 20th April 2019.

24
    a.   (Jan. 3, 2019) Gamification Market: Global Industry Size, Trends and Forecast 2026 by Credence Research. Available: http://www.abnews wire.com/pressreleases/gamification-market-global-industry-size-trends-and-forecast-2026-by-credence-research_311509.html. Last accessed 20th April 2019.

    b.   (Aug. 2017) Global Gamification Market 2017–2021. Available: https://www.technavio.com/report/global-gamification-market. Last accessed 20th April 2019.

    c.   (2018) Gamification Market – Growth, Trends, and Forecast (2019–2024). Available: https://www.mordorintelligence.com/industry-reports/gamification-market. Last accessed 20th April 2019.

    d.   (2016) Gamification Market. Available: https://www.psmarketresearch.com/market-analysis/gamification-market. Last accessed 20th April 2019.

25   (2016) Gamification Market. Available: https://www.psmarketresearch.com/market-analysis/gamification-market. Last accessed 20th April 2019.

26   McGonigal, J., (2011) *Reality is Broken: Why Games Make Us Better and How They Can Change the World.* The Penguin Group, pp. 15.

27   (2010) How Playboy Seduced Fans on Facebook. Available: http://www.bunchball.com/customers/playboy-miss-social. Last accessed 20th April 2019.

28   Olds, J. and Milner, P. (1954) 'Positive reinforcement produced by electrical stimulation of septal area and other regions of rat brain'. *Journal of Comparative and Physiological Psychology,* 47(6), 419–427.

29   Pavlov, I. P. (1928) *Lectures on Conditioned Reflexes.* (Translated by W.H. Gantt) London: Allen and Unwin.

30   Skinner, B. F. (1938) *The Behavior of Organisms: An Experimental Analysis.* New York: Appleton-Century-Crofts.

31   Knutson, B. and Samanez-Larkin, G. R. (2012) Brain, Decision, and Debt. In R. Brubaker, R. M. Lawless and C. J. Tabb (Eds) *A Debtor World: Interdisciplinary Perspectives on Debt.* New York: Oxford University Press, pp. 167–180.

32   Eyal, N. (2014) *Hooked: How to Build Habit-Forming Products.* USA, Penguin.

33 Kahneman, D. (2011) *Thinking, Fast and Slow*. Farrar, Straus & Giroux.

34 (Feb. 8, 2016) Blend It: 6 Remarkable Lessons From this Record Setting Campaign. Available: https://digitalsparkmarketing.com/blend-it/. Last accessed 20th April 2019.

35 Herzberg, F., Mausner, B. and Snyderman, B. (1959) *The Motivation to Work*. (2nd ed.) New York: John Wiley.

36 Vroom, V. H. and Deci, E. L. (1983) *Management and Motivation*. (First published 1970) Penguin.

37 Kahneman, D., Knetsch, J. L. and Thaler, R. H. (1990) 'Experimental tests of the Endowment Effect and the Coase Theorem'. *Journal of Political Economy*, 98(6), 1325–1348.

38 Maslow, A. (1943) 'A Theory of Human Motivation.' *Psychological Review*, 50(4).

39 Maslow, A. (1964) *Motivation and Personality*. New York, NY: Harper.

40 Pink, D. H. (2010) *Drive: The Surprising Truth About What Motivates Us*. Canongate Books.

41 Deci, E. L. Flaste, R. (1995) *Why We Do What We Do*. USA, Penguin Books.

42 Eyal, N. (2014) *Hooked: How to Build Habit-Forming Products*. USA: Penguin.

43 Pink, D. H. (2010) *Drive: The Surprising Truth About What Motivates Us*. Canongate Books, pp. 144.

44 Campbell, J. (2012) *The Hero with a Thousand Faces (The Collected Works of Joseph Campbell)*. New World Library.

45 (2018) Duolingo. Available: https://www.duolingo.com/. Last accessed 20th April 2019.

46 (Aug. 12, 2015) Gamified Design Review: An In-depth Analysis of Duolingo. Available: http://www.gamification.co/2015/08/12/gamified-design-review-a-in-depth-analysis-of-duolingo/. Last accessed 20th April 2019

47 Deci, E. L. and Flaste, R. (1995) *Why We Do What We Do*. USA: Penguin Books, pp. 66.

48 Vygotsky, L. (Apr. 18, 2019) Zone of Proximal Development. Available: https://en.wikipedia.org/wiki/Zone_of_proximal_development. Last accessed 20th April 2019.

49 (Apr. 8, 2019) ROWE. Available https://en.wikipedia.org/wiki/ROWE. Last accessed 20th April 2019.

50   (2019) ShipIt. Available: https://www.atlassian.com/company/shipit. Last accessed 20th April 2019.

51   (2019) FedEx Day: Lighting Corporate Passion. https://www.scrum.org/resources/fedex-day-lighting-corporate-passion. Last accessed 20th April 2019.

52   Chou, Y. K. (2015) *Actionable Gamification: Beyond Points, Badges, and Leaderboards*. Octalysis Media, pp. 131.

53   (2019) Superbetter. Available: https://www.superbetter.com/. Last accessed 20th April 2019.

54   Gee, J. P. (2007) *What Video Games Have to Teach Us About Learning and Literacy*. New York, Palgrave Macmillan, pp. 54.

55   Chou, Y. K. (2015) *Actionable Gamification: Beyond Points, Badges, and Leaderboards*. Octalysis Media, pp. 312.

56   Kahneman, D. (2015) *Thinking, Fast and Slow*. Penguin Books, pp. 283–285.

57   Schwartz, P. (1979) *The Emergent Paradigm: Changing Patterns of Thought and Belief*. Sri International.

58   (Apr. 18, 2019) Zone of Proximal Development. Vygotsky, L. Available: https://en.wikipedia.org/wiki/Zone_of_proximal_development.   Last accessed 20th April 2019.

59   Csikszentmihalyi, M. (2002) *Flow: The Classic Work On How to Achieve Happiness*. Rider.

60   (2019) LootCrate. Available: https://www.lootcrate.com/. Last accessed 20th April 2019.

61   (2018) HiddenCity. Available: https://www.inthehiddencity.com/. Last accessed 20th April 2019.

62   (Dec. 3, 2014) Loyalty Case Study: jetBlue's True Blue Rewards. Available: https://blog.smile.io/loyalty-case-study-jetblue-airline-rewards.   Last accessed 20th April 2019.

63   (Apr. 6, 2019) Growth-share Matrix. Available: https://en.wikipedia.org/wiki/Growth-share_matrix. Last accessed 20th April 2019.

64   (Apr. 8, 2019) Porter's Five Forces Analysis. Available: https://en.wikipedia.org/wiki/Porter%27s_five_forces_analysis. Last accessed 20th April 2019.

65   (Apr. 3, 2019) SWOT Analysis. Available: https://en.wikipedia.org/wiki/SWOT_analysis. Last accessed 20th April 2019.

66   (Mar. 6, 2019) PEST Analysis. Available: https://en.wikipedia.org/wiki/PEST_analysis. Last accessed 20th April 2019.

67 (Jul. 10, 2017) So, What is a Trailblazer?. Available: https://www.salesforce.com/blog/2017/07/so-what-is-a-trailblazer.html. Last accessed 20th April 2019.

68 Fitocracy. Available https://www.fitocracy.com/about-us/. Last accessed 7th June 2019.

69 (Mar. 4, 2018) How to Score Leads for Values Alignment. Available: https://www.boundless.ai/blog/how-to-score-leads-for-values-alignment/. Last accessed 20th April 2019.

70 Marczewski, A. (2015) User Types. In *Even Ninja Monkeys Like to Play: Gamification, Game Thinking and Motivational Design*. (1st ed.) CreateSpace Independent Publishing Platform, pp. 65–80.

71 Radoff, J. (2011) *Game On: Energize your Business with Social Media Games*. Wiley Publishing, Inc., pp 81.

72 Campbell, J. (2008) *The Hero With a Thousand Faces*. New World Library.

73 (2019) Beaconing Project. Available: http://beaconing.eu/insights/the-whys/. Last accessed 20th April 2019.

74 Rogers, E. (2003) *Diffusion of Innovations*. (5th ed.) Simon and Schuster.

75 (May 2, 2018) Gamification in Education: 4 Ways to Bring Games to Your Classroom. Available: https://tophat.com/blog/gamification-education-class/. Last accessed 20th April 2019.

76 Case Study – BBVA Game. Available: https://subscription.packtpub.com/book/business/9781783000203/1/ch01lvl2sec05/case-study-bbva-game. Last accessed 20th April 2019.

77 (May 12, 2010) Shadow-Activated QR Code Actually Useful and Cool. Available: https://www.adweek.com/creativity/shadow-activated-qr-code-actually-useful-and-cool-139975/. Last accessed 20th April 2019.

78 Chou, Y. K. (2015) *Actionable Gamification: Beyond Points, Badges, and Leaderboards*. Octalysis Media.

79 Gee, J. P. (2007) *What Video Games Have to Teach Us About Learning and Literacy*. Palgrave Macmillan, pp. 137.

80 Csikszentmihalyi, M. (2002) *Flow: The Classic Work on How to Achieve Happiness*. Rider.

81 (2019) Beachbody. Available: https://www.beachbody.com/. Last accessed 20th April 2019.

82 Gee, J. P. (2007) *What Video Games Have To Teach Us About Learning and Literacy*. Palgrave Macmillan, pp. 25.

83 (Apr. 13, 2019) Sun Wukong. Available: https://en.wikipedia.org/wiki/ Sun_Wukong. Last accessed 20th April 2019.

84 (Aug. 6, 2015)The 8 Best Easter Eggs on Google Maps. Available: http:// www.collegehumor.com/post/7028762/10-easter-eggs-you-can-find-on- google-maps. Last accessed 20th April 2019.

85 (Dec. 27, 2018) 65 Funny Things to Ask Siri for a Good Giggle. Available: https://www.pocket-lint.com/apps/news/apple/134568-funny-things- to-ask-siri-best-things-to-ask-siri-for-a-giggle. Last accessed 20th April 2019.

86 (Oct. 10, 2011) The Personal Tributes to Steve Jobs Around the World. Available: https://www.theatlantic.com/technology/archive/2011/10/ personal-tributes-steve-jobs-around-world/337035/. Last accessed 20th April 2019.

87 (Dec. 3, 2015) How to Choose the Right UX Metrics for Your Product. Available: https://library.gv.com/how-to-choose-the-right-ux-metrics- for-your-product-5f46359ab5be. Last accessed 20th April 2019.

88 (2019) Design Sprint Methodology. Available: https://designsprintkit. withgoogle.com/methods/. Last accessed 20th April 2019.

Bibliography – Further Reading and Resources

Books

Berger, J. (2014) *Contagious: How to Build Word of Mouth in the Digital Age.* UK: Simon & Schuster.

Bogost, I. (2016) *Play Anything: The Pleasure of Limits, the Uses of Boredom, & the Secrets of Games.* NY: Basic Books.

Brown, S. (2010) *Play: How it Shapes the Brain, Opens the Imagination, and Invigorates the Soul.* USA: Penguin Group Avery.

Burke, B. (2014) *Gamify: How Gamification Motivates People to Do Extraordinary Things.* Routledge.

Campbell, J. (2012) *The Hero with a Thousand Faces (The Collected Works of Joseph Campbell).* New World Library.

Chou, Y. K. (2015) *Actionable Gamification: Beyond Points, Badges, and Leaderboards.* Octalysis Media.

Csikszentmihalyi, M. (2002) *Flow: The Classic Work on How to Achieve Happiness.* Rider.

Deci, E. L. and Flaste, R. (1995) *Why We Do What We Do.* USA: Penguin Books.

Eyal, N. (2014). *Hooked: How to Build Habit-Forming Products.* USA: Penguin.

Gee, J. P. (2007) *What Video Games Have to Teach Us About Learning and Literacy.* New York: Palgrave Macmillan.

Herzberg, F., Mausner, B. and Snyderman, B. (1959) *The Motivation to Work.* (2nd ed.) New York: John Wiley.

Huizinga, J. (1950) *Homo Ludens: A Study of the Play-Element in Culture.* Roy Publishers.

Kahneman, D. (2011) *Thinking, Fast and Slow.* Farrar, Straus & Giroux.

Kahneman, D. Knetsch, J. L. and Thaler, R. H. (1990) 'Experimental tests of the Endowment Effect and the Coase Theorem'. *Journal of Political Economy.* 98(6), 1325–1348.

Kapp, K. M. (2014) *The Gamification of Learning and Instruction Fieldbook: Ideas into Practice.* John Wiley & Sons.

Kim, A. J. (2018) *Game Thinking: Innovate Smarter & Drive Deep Engagement with Design Techniques from Hit Games*. (2nd ed.) Gamethinking.io.

Knutson, B. and Samanez-Larkin, G. R. (2012) Brain, Decision, and Debt. In R. Brubaker, R. M. Lawless and C. J. Tabb (Eds) *A Debtor World: Interdisciplinary Perspectives on Debt*. New York: Oxford University Press.

Marczewski, A. (2015) *Even Ninja Monkeys Like to Play: Gamification, Game Thinking and Motivational Design*. (1st ed.) CreateSpace Independent Publishing Platform.

Maslow, A. (1943) 'A Theory of Human Motivation.' *Psychological Review*, 50(4).

Maslow, A. (1964) *Motivation and Personality*. New York, NY: Harper.

McGonigal, J. (2011) *Reality is Broken: Why Games Make Us Better and How They Can Change the World*. The Penguin Group.

Olds, J. and Milner, P. (1954) 'Positive reinforcement produced by electrical stimulation of septal area and other regions of rat brain.' *Journal of Comparative and Physiological Psychology*, 47(6), 419–427.

Pavlov, I. P. (1928) *Lectures on Conditioned Reflexes*. (Translated by W.H. Gantt) London: Allen and Unwin.

Pink, D. H. (2009) *Drive: The Surprising Truth About What Motivates Us*. USA: Riverhead Hardcover.

Radoff, J. (2011) *Game On: Energize Your Business with Social Media Games*. Wiley Publishing, Inc.

Rogers, E. (2003) *Diffusion of Innovations*. (5th ed.) Simon and Schuster.

Rollings, A. and Morris, D. (2003) *Game Architecture and Design: A New Edition*. (1st ed.) New Riders.

Routledge, H. (2016) *Why Games Are Good For Business: How to Leverage the Power of Serious Games, Gamification and Simulations*. (1st ed.) Palgrave Macmillan.

Schell, J. (2015) *The Art of Game Design: A Book of Lenses*. (2nd ed.) CRC Press; Taylor & Francis Group.

Skinner, B. F. (1938) *The Behavior of Organisms: An Experimental Analysis*. New York: Appleton-Century-Crofts.

Schwartz, P. (1979) *The Emergent Paradigm: Changing Patterns of Thought and Belief*. Sri International.

Suits, B. (2005) *The Grasshopper: Games, Life and Utopia*. Broadview Press.

Sutton-Smith, B. (2001) *The Ambiguity of Play*. USA: Harvard University Press.

Thaler, R. H. (2016) *Misbehaving: The Making of Behavioural Economics*. UK: Penguin Random House.

Vroom, V. H. and Deci, E. L. (1983) *Management and Motivation*. (First published 1970) Penguin.

Walz, S. P. et al. (2015) *The Gameful World: Approaches, Issues, Applications*. USA: MIT Press.

Werbach, K. (2012) *For the Win: How Game Thinking Can Revolutionize Your Business*. Wharton Digital Press.

Websites

aeStranger. Available: https://aestranger.com. Last accessed 20th April 2019.

Dr Zac Fitz-Walter. Available: http://zacfitzwalter.com/. Last accessed 20th April 2019.

Gamification Europe. Available: https://gamification-europe.com/. Last accessed 20th April 2019.

Gamification Nation. Available: https://www.gamificationnation.com. Last accessed 20th April 2019.

Gamification+. Available: https://gamificationplus.uk/. Last accessed 20th April 2019.

Game Thinking. Available: https://gamethinking.io/. Last accessed 20th April 2019.

Gamified UK: Thoughts on Gamification and more. Available: https://www.gamified.uk/. Last accessed 20th April 2019.

Strategic Innovation Lab. Available: https://strategicinnovationlab.com/. Last accessed 20th April 2019.

Yu-Kai Chou. Octalysis Framework. Available: https://yukaichou.com/. Last accessed 20th April 2019.

Index